Sacred Sensuality: A Guide to sex Magic and spiritual Awakening

Transforming Intimacy into a path of Enlightenment

Maya Reynolds

Table of Contents

INTRODUCTION

In a world often dominated by hurried routines and superficial connections, there exists a profound and transformative realm waiting to be explored—one where sensuality intertwines with spirituality, and intimacy becomes a conduit for profound awakening. Welcome to "Sacred Sensuality: A Guide to Sex Magic and Spiritual Awakening," where we embark on a journey that transcends the conventional boundaries of both our physical and spiritual lives.

is not merely a guide; it is an invitation to rediscover

the spiritual essence inherent in human sexuality and to harness its transformative potential. As we delve into the realms of sex magic and spiritual awakening, we will unravel the ancient wisdom that views intimacy as a sacred path leading to enlightenment.

The intersection of sensuality and spirituality is not a

new concept; it is an age-old understanding that has been revered in various cultures throughout history. This book aims to reintroduce and demystify these ancient practices, offering a contemporary perspective on how the fusion of sexuality and spirituality can lead to profound personal and spiritual growth.

Throughout the chapters, we will explore the principles

of sex magic, the energetic dynamics of intimacy, and the alchemical transformation that occurs when we approach our relationships with mindfulness and intention. From rituals that deepen connection to the empowering aspects of embracing personal desires, each section is designed to guide you toward a more profound understanding of yourself and your relationships.

Our exploration is not without its challenges, and we will

navigate the complexities of desire, attachment, and

societal conditioning. By doing so, we pave the way for personal empowerment and the integration of sacred sensuality into our daily lives.

Embark on this journey with an open heart and a willingness to transform. "Sacred Sensuality" is an odyssey into the depths of human connection—a guidebook for those seeking to transcend the ordinary and embrace the extraordinary in the union of body, mind, and spirit. Together, let us embark on the transformative path of enlightenment through the sacred realms of sensuality.

CHAPTER I

The Spiritual Essence of Sexuality

Exploring the spiritual dimension of human sexuality

Beyond the world of the physical, human sexuality, which is a complicated and multi-faceted component of our existence, extends considerably beyond. There is a fundamental and frequently ignored layer that lies beneath the surface of carnal wants, and these desires are spiritual. This essay dives into investigating the spiritual facet of human sexuality to illuminate the more significant links between the physical manifestations of intimacy that we engage in and the vast realms of spirituality.

The spiritual aspect of human sexuality recognizes, at its foundation, that our bodies are not only vessels for the experience of physical pleasure; instead, they are also carriers of heavenly energy. Numerous historical traditions, ranging from Tantra to Hinduism and beyond, have consistently acknowledged the spiritual value of sexual energy for a considerable amount of time. A connection that transcends the physical to unite individuals on a profound spiritual level is a holy ritual in these traditions. The act of making love is considered to be a sacred ritual.

To investigate the spiritual aspect of human sexuality, it is necessary to know about the connectivity that exists between our sexual experiences and the more significant spiritual journey that we are on. To accomplish this, a shift in viewpoint is required, one that goes beyond the societal conditioning that frequently restricts our sense of sexuality to the act of physical contact alone. Individuals can unleash the potential for personal and spiritual growth through close interactions if they adopt a broader perspective.

The body is considered to be a sacred temple in several different spiritual traditions, and sexual energy is regarded as a powerful force that, when actively harnessed, has the potential to raise one's level of consciousness. Tantra, for example, emphasizes sexuality as a means to achieve enlightenment on a spiritual level. Practitioners are encouraged to engage in lovemaking with mindfulness and intention, recognizing the divine within themselves and their partners, and to do so within the context of lovemaking. Tantra is a discipline that combines the dualistic components of reality, such as male and female, Shiva and Shakti, in a harmonious dance of energy.

In addition, the spiritual aspect of human sexuality emphasizes the significance of establishing a connection with one's own body and desires. In a world where societal conventions frequently govern what is acceptable or forbidden, individuals may discover that they have become estranged from their true selves. It is possible to begin on a path of self-discovery by investigating the spiritual element of sexuality. This allows one to accept and embrace their wants without passing judgment on that acceptance.

Additionally, the concept of sacred sensuality is brought to the forefront as a result of the incorporation of spirituality with human sexuality. This concept entails treating the experience of intimacy as one that is both sacred and transformational. Individuals are encouraged to create a deeper connection with their partners, considering each meeting as a chance for spiritual communion. This is a result of the fact that it does this. In sacred sensuality, the act of making love is raised to the level of a spiritual practice, which helps to cultivate emotional closeness and transcends the constraints of the ego.

The spiritual side of human sexuality is not limited to particular religious views; instead, it is a facet of our human experience shared by everyone everywhere. It invites people from all walks of life to investigate the intrinsic link between their bodies, thoughts, and personalities. Individuals can have energy and wisdom that has the potential to enhance not only their relationships but also their general sense of well-being if they take this course of action.

It is of the utmost importance to recognize that the investigation of the spiritual aspect of human sexuality is a journey that is both highly individual and highly subjective. One person's idea of what constitutes spirituality may be fundamentally different from that of another. The richness and complexity of human sexuality are highlighted by this diversity, which also highlights the necessity of adopting an attitude that is open and non-judgmental to comprehend and embrace the spiritual dimensions of intimacy.

In conclusion, investigating the spiritual aspect of human sexuality provides a path to profound self-discovery, significant personal development, and enlightenment on a spiritual level. It invites individuals to recognize the divine element of human connection, transcending the physical and societal limits on personal relationships. Individuals can harness the transforming potential within themselves by embracing the spiritual components of sexuality. This allows them to cultivate deeper connections with their partners and embark on a journey toward a more profound awareness of both the self and the divine.

Historical perspectives on sacred sexuality

Throughout human history, the investigation of holy sexuality has traversed the annals of human history, weaving together a rich tapestry of varied cultural beliefs, rituals, and practices that perceive the union of sexuality and spirituality as a sacred and transcendent experience. The great significance of human sexuality as a conduit for spiritual connection and enlightenment has been recognized by communities throughout the ages and across civilizations. These societies have faced the challenge of navigating the complex relationship between the physical and the metaphysical throughout history.

In ancient civilizations, particularly in Mesopotamia and Egypt, the worship of fertility deities clearly indicated the intertwining of sexuality and spirituality. Not only did these societies acknowledge the significance of sexuality in the life cycle, but they also honored the heavenly energies that were involved with reproduction. The temples that were devoted to fertility deities frequently became places where rituals were performed that included sexual actions as sacred rites. These ceremonies emphasized the link between earthly wants and divine forces.

There are profound insights into the historical viewpoints on sacred sexuality that may be found in the ancient Hindu scriptures, particularly the Vedas and the Tantras. For example, the union of Shiva and Shakti represents the divine in Hinduism, which frequently depicts the holy as both male and female. In order to emphasize the inescapable connection between masculine and feminine energies, this heavenly union serves as a metaphor for the cosmic dance responsible for maintaining the cosmos. Tantric rituals, which have their origins in Hinduism, investigate the esoteric aspects of sexuality and view it as a potent force for spiritual transformation. Tantric practitioners attempt to harness sexual energy to awaken the dormant spiritual potential that lies within them. This is accomplished via the use of rituals and meditated practices.

Moving westward, we find that ancient Greece offers another historical perspective through which we can investigate sacred sexuality. Aphrodite, the goddess of Greek mythology, represented love and beauty and the sensual aspects of human existence. She was also the goddess of beauty. Within the philosophical debate known as the Symposium, credited to Plato, the concept of Eros, the divine energy of love and desire, is investigated. A holistic approach to spirituality that considers the physical sphere is suggested by the fact that the search for higher knowledge and beauty is connected with the feeling of passionate love within this discourse.

A poetic celebration of love and sexuality, the Song of Solomon may be found in the Hebrew Bible. For this reason, it is considered an essential part of the mystical traditions of Judaism. The Song of Solomon is interpreted in various ways, but most scholars believe it is an allegory for the divine love between God and the soul. An awareness of the sacredness of physical love and its symbolic connection to the sacred is reflected in the lyrics through the rich imagery and sensuality that they include.

Another viewpoint on the combination of sensuality and spirituality can be found in the Taoist philosophy prevalent in ancient China. Yin and Yang is a notion that is central to Taoism. It symbolizes the duality and interconnectedness of all things, including the male and feminine energies. The purpose of Taoist sexual practices, such as the art of "bedchamber alchemy," is to facilitate the cultivation and circulation of sexual energy to achieve health, longevity, and spiritual enlightenment. A holistic approach to human existence that considers both the material and spiritual components is fostered by Taoist teachings, which emphasize the importance of maintaining balance and harmony throughout their entirety.

As the Middle Ages progressed, the troubadour tradition in medieval Europe gave rise to a literary investigation of courtly love. This was a sophisticated and intricate statement of romantic and spiritual devotion. Even though it did not specifically center on sexuality, courtly love frequently involved a profound emotional and spiritual connection between the two people involved. Not only did the troubadours' lyrical works praise the transformational power of love, but they also elevated it beyond the sphere of physical significance and into the realm of spiritual significance.

During the Renaissance, there was a renaissance of

interest in esoteric traditions and classical knowledge, which led to a fresh investigation into the mystical aspects of human sexuality. Figures such as Marsilio Ficino, a philosopher who lived during the Renaissance, investigated love's symbolic and spiritual elements. The formation of Western esoteric traditions was impacted by the writings of Ficino, which focused on the transformative power of love and its relationship to the divine soul.

A renaissance of interest in holy sexuality occurred

during the 19th and 20th centuries, particularly within Western esoteric and occult societies for the most part. Some individuals investigated the incorporation of sexuality into magical techniques, such as Aleister Crowley, who was a notable occultist. Thelema, which was Crowley's spiritual theory, placed a strong emphasis on the need for sexual liberty and the utilization of sexual energy for spiritual advancement.

Sacred sexuality has been brought back into prominence

in recent decades as a result of the New Age movement and the resurrection of interest in old spiritual traditions. Tantra, a practice that originated in ancient India, has gained popularity as individuals seek to merge spirituality and sexuality in a contemporary setting. Tantra is one example of such a practice. Old knowledge is aligned with current ethical considerations through the modern exploration of holy sexuality, which frequently emphasizes permission, communication, and awareness.

A rich and diverse tapestry of beliefs and practices that

respect the intrinsic relationship between human sexuality and spirituality is revealed by the historical viewpoints on sacred sexuality, as stated in the conclusion. Communities have acknowledged the transforming power of embracing the holy within the intimate throughout a wide range of cultures and historical periods. The historical path of sacred sexuality reveals a recurring knowledge that the physical and the spiritual are not mutually exclusive but rather interconnected aspects of the human experience. This understanding can be found in ancient temples' rites and the esoteric practices of mystical traditions. This historical investigation serves as a reminder that the connection between sexuality and spirituality has been a source of inspiration, reflection, and transcendence throughout the ages. We should keep this in mind as we negotiate the difficulties of modern life.

The significance of embracing sensuality on the spiritual path

When one sets out on a spiritual journey, they frequently find themselves navigating the complex regions of their selves to gain a more profound comprehension of existence and establish a relationship with the divine. In this pursuit of spiritual enlightenment, embracing sensuality is a fundamental and transformational feature that must be considered. When it comes to unlocking spiritual insights, encouraging self-discovery, and building a more profound connection with the holy, sensuality acts as a gateway. Sensuality is frequently associated with heightened awareness of the senses and the physical body.

On the spiritual path, the recognition that the physical body is not only a vessel to be transcended but rather a vehicle through which spiritual experiences might develop is at the core of the practice of embracing sensuality. Throughout human history, numerous spiritual traditions have dealt with the question of how the physical and the spiritual are related to one another, frequently acknowledging the inherent connection between the two. As the spiritual journey expands, the body, with all its senses and desires, becomes a canvas upon which it presents itself.

Several Eastern religions, like Buddhism and Hinduism, emphasize the concept of mindfulness and awareness of the present moment as an essential component of their spiritual practices. In this discussion, embracing sensuality means being fully present in the experience of the senses, whether it be the flavor of food, the sensation of the breeze, or the touch of a person you care about. Individuals can gain a heightened awareness of the present moment by cultivating mindfulness in sensuous sensations. This is a crucial component of many different spiritual traditions.

It is also important to note that sensuality plays a significant part in investigating Tantra, a spiritual tradition that began in ancient India. Tantra is a spiritual practice that considers the world to be a manifestation of the divine. Tantra also finds the body and sexual experiences to be routes to the sacred. For transcending dualities and experiencing the union of the material and spiritual realms, practitioners of techniques such as Tantric yoga and holy sexuality strive to achieve this transformation. Tantra is a practice that involves embracing pleasure to establish a connection with the divine energy that permeates every facet of life.

Sensuality is frequently linked to the concept of the sacred feminine in the mystical traditions prevalent in Western cultures. Acknowledging the divine feminine principle emphasizes the significance of intuition, receptivity, and nurturing qualities of the self. When one embraces sensuality, it becomes a means of honoring and connecting with the feminine's inherent holiness, whether represented in the form of the goddess or as an archetype within the individual.

Regarding the spiritual path, the relevance of embracing sensuality extends beyond the person and encompasses interactions and ties with other people. When approached with mindfulness and an open heart, intimate relationships offer spiritual growth and mutual transformation possibilities. Both parties can benefit from these opportunities. As a result of holy connections, the exchange of physical intimacy goes beyond simple pleasure. It develops into a voyage of exploration and spiritual communion that both parties enjoy.

In addition, the acceptance of sensuality is congruent with embodied spirituality, which emphasizes the connection between the spiritual and physical components of human existence. With all of its sensations and wants, the body is not seen as something that stands in the way of spiritual advancement; rather, it is seen as a vehicle through which the soul can fully experience and express itself. Individuals can access the wisdom of their bodies by embracing sensuality. This allows them to listen to the messages their bodies send them and match their spiritual practice with the rhythms inherent to their existence.

In addition, sensuality acts as a catalyst for self-acceptance and self-discovery along the spiritual path. In a culture that frequently imposes societal standards and expectations on the body and desire, embracing sensuality becomes an act of reclaiming one's authentic self rather than a way to conform to those expectations. Recognizing sensations and desires as vital components of the human experience rather than as distractions is a necessary step on the path. This requires examining and accepting the whole gamut of sensory experiences and desires. Individuals can liberate themselves from feelings of shame, guilt, or cultural conditioning that may have impeded their spiritual development through acceptance.

In addition, the teachings of current spiritual teachers and practitioners make it clear that the value of embracing sensuality on the spiritual path is becoming increasingly apparent. The modern period has seen the emergence of voices that advocate for the integration of sensuality and spirituality. These voices emphasize the significance of a holistic approach to the spiritual journey. Authors, presenters, and spiritual advisors encourage individuals to consider their bodies sacred. They are also encouraged to engage in rituals that celebrate sensuality to maintain a connection with the divine both within and without themselves.

On the other hand, it is necessary to travel the route of pleasure while staying conscious and considering ethical considerations. In the context of the spiritual path, the significance of embracing sensuality does not entail unbridled indulgence in hedonistic pleasures. Instead, it invites one to connect with the senses consciously and intentionally while simultaneously acknowledging the holiness inherent in every experience. To practice mindful sensuality, one must exercise discernment, ensuring that their activities are by ethical values and contribute to the well-being of themselves and others.

The significance of embracing sensuality on the spiritual path is multifaceted and rich in its implications for personal development, connection with the divine, and the evolution of awareness. In conclusion, the significance of this is multifaceted and rich in its implications. Recognizing that sensuality is not incompatible with spirituality, but rather, when addressed with mindfulness and intention, becomes a profound avenue for spiritual study. The common thread runs through all of these different types of spiritual viewpoints, whether anchored in Eastern traditions, mystical teachings, or contemporary spiritual perspectives. Honoring the body, growing awareness of the present moment, and navigating intimate connections with regard are all components of embracing sensuality. Accepting sensuality acts as a beacon, illuminating a more complete and holistic experience of the divine and the self for those just beginning their journey toward spiritual enlightenment.

CHAPTER II

Understanding Sex Magic

Defining sex magic and its roots in ancient traditions

The word "sex magic," which may arouse curiosity or even suspicion, refers to a complex and esoteric discipline with roots in many old traditions. Understanding sex magic is like taking a historical trip through the ages to discover the transforming and mystical components of human sexuality that have been used for spiritual advancement. Sex magic is fundamentally a ceremonial technique in which sexual energy is purposefully used for magical or spiritual purposes. This essay aims to explain sex magic, explore its historical origins, and highlight the practice's transforming and sacred qualities.

The roots of sex magic can be found in prehistoric societies when the fusion of spirituality and sensuality was celebrated rather than hidden in mystery. Sexual rituals were essential to religious ceremonies in ancient Egypt, Mesopotamia, and India. These cultures also commonly equated sexual rituals with fertility, regeneration, and the divine balance of male and feminine energies. Sex magical rituals were increasingly organized as a result of the widespread notion that sexual energy contained a vital life force and could be a channel for spiritual power in these communities.

Ancient Sumerian scriptures contain one of the first known accounts of sex magic, as they describe sacred prostitution as a widespread practice in fertility goddess temples. These priestesses believed that the energy produced by these rites would guarantee agricultural prosperity and wealth, so they committed sexual acts as offerings to the gods. Similarly, sexual rites representing the marriage of the divine couple were a part of the worship of Isis and Osiris in ancient Egypt, reflecting the cyclical nature of life, death, and rebirth.

Sex magic has its roots in Hinduism as well, especially in the Tantric tradition. Tantra, which translates as "to weave" or "to expand," is a broad category of mystical activities that bring together the individual and the divine. One of the main themes in Tantric traditions is the merger of Shiva and Shakti, the masculine and female cosmic powers. Tantra seeks to transform sexual energy through rituals, meditations, and sexual practices, leading its adherents toward enlightenment and spiritual awakening. Tantric traditions are numerous and varied, but they all recognize the sacredness of sexual energy and its capacity for spiritual development. This is a commonality among them.

The Greco-Roman mystery religions introduced sexuality into their religious rituals when they arrived in the ancient Mediterranean region. The Eleusinian Mysteries were devoted to the goddess Demeter, including initiation rites with sacred sexual practices. The initiates thought that by having intercourse during the ceremonies, they would be able to learn more about the mysteries and the truths about life and death.

The concept of the sacred marriage serves as a means of exploring sex magic within the esoteric traditions of the Kabbalah, a branch of Jewish mysticism. The Sephirot Tiferet and Shekhinah, which symbolize the union of the divine masculine and feminine, are thought to reflect the cosmic order. Practitioners who seek heavenly illumination and spiritual insight align with the harmonious balance of these forces.

Sex magic was reexamined during the Renaissance due to the resurgence of interest in Western esotericism. Renowned scholars like Heinrich Cornelius Agrippa and Giordano Bruno investigated the esoteric facets of sexuality, viewing it as a powerful tool for spiritual and magical endeavors. A defining feature of Western mystical traditions was blending alchemical principles with sexual symbolism to highlight the transformational potential that arises from the union of opposites.

Prominent occultists emerged in the 19th and 20th centuries, advancing and popularizing sex magic. Aleister Crowley, a controversial but significant figure in Western esotericism, included sex magic in his magical system, Thelema. Writings by Crowley, especially in books like "The Book of the Law," stress the significance of sexual liberty and the deliberate application of sexual energy to magical ends. Thelema uses rituals for both solo and group sex magic, emphasizing the directed will and imagination during intercourse.

The interpretation and use of sex magic in the modern day have changed as a result of the impact of numerous spiritual and occult traditions. Many contemporary practitioners modify and incorporate sex magic into their spiritual frameworks, drawing inspiration from traditional teachings. Some present-day practitioners of sex magic emphasize consent, ethical issues, and a holistic view of sexuality. They examine the practice within the framework of Wicca, modern paganism, or eclectic magical traditions.

The historical foundations of sex magic are significant, but so is its capacity for spiritual and emotional growth. The core of the practice is the deliberate and conscious use of sexual energy to enhance magical processes, be they for manifestation, healing, or divine communication. Sex magicians aim to reach higher realms of awareness and transcend the mundane by harmonizing the physical and spiritual facets of human existence.

Sex magic's historical roots offer a foundation, but it's essential to acknowledge the variety of viewpoints and methods found in this esoteric field. The way that sex magic is interpreted and used varies wildly, depending on the personal and cultural situations in which it is practiced. Furthermore, the ethical issues surrounding sex magic—consent, decency, and awareness, for example—highlight the significance of using this potent and transformational technique responsibly and thoughtfully.

Understanding the historical foundations of sex magic and recognizing its multifarious expressions throughout cultures and eras are essential to defining it. Sex magic has always been a part of human spirituality, from the esoteric practices of Western occultists to the sacred ceremonies of ancient civilizations. The relevance of sex magic remains in its ability to unite the spiritual and physical realms, providing a means of achieving profound self-discovery, magical empowerment, and spiritual illumination, even as practitioners continue to study and modify this age-old practice.

Practical applications of sex magic for spiritual growth

Sex magic is a powerful and esoteric technique that, when used with intention and consciousness, can be a transformational instrument for spiritual growth. However, it is sometimes buried in mystery and misconceptions. Sex magic is essentially the deliberate use of sexual energy to accomplish particular magical or spiritual goals. This essay explores how sex magic can be used for personal and spiritual development by delving into the practical aspects of this age-old and sometimes misunderstood discipline.

Using sexual energy as a potent manifestation catalyst is one of the main real-world uses for sex magic. In magic, intention is everything. Sex magic uses the energy produced during sexual climax and desire to enhance the power of intentions. The elevated state of arousal provides an intense, concentrated surge of energy that can be focused on a particular objective or desire. To infuse their sexual energy with intention, practitioners perform rituals that frequently include mantra chanting and visualization. With this deliberate concentration, sex magic becomes a powerful tool for manifesting goals, whether they have to do with spiritual accomplishment, career success, or personal development.

Moreover, sex magic provides a route to elevated consciousness and spiritual bliss. Through the integration of sexual practices with meditation techniques, practitioners can reach transcendent realms of awareness. In particular, tantric traditions stress the use of sexual energy to reawaken the inner spiritual potential that has lain dormant. People can transcend the limits of conventional consciousness and experience a merger of the physical and spiritual through extended and focused lovemaking combined with breathwork and imagery. This altered condition is considered a gateway to deep spiritual understanding, self-awareness, and a direct line of communication with God.

The field of physical and energetic healing is another real-world application of sex magic. Chakras, or the body's energy centers, are important concepts in many spiritual traditions. These energy centers can be activated, balanced, and cleansed using sex magic, which enhances general wellbeing and wellbeing. It is possible to intentionally target particular chakras with sexual activities to alleviate emotional and energetic imbalances. For example, during sexual rituals, focusing on the heart chakra may help heal emotional wounds and awaken the heart to love and compassion.

When used mindfully, sexual energy can also be a powerful tool for overcoming trauma and emotional blocks. Through the release and transmutation of pent-up emotional energy, sex magic rituals can support a cathartic process that lets people face and let go of unresolved feelings. Practitioners may discover a holistic approach to their wellbeing by including psychological and emotional healing in sexual practices, which can lead to a stronger sense of inner harmony and emotional resilience.

In addition, sex magic practices' deliberate development and circulation of sexual energy are consistent with traditional Eastern practices, especially those found in Tantra and Taoism. According to these traditions, sexual energy is the essential life force (prana or chi) that can enhance longevity, wellbeing, and spiritual awakening by harnessing and distributing it throughout the body. In Taoist practices, methods like the microcosmic orbit include directing sexual energy along energy meridians in order to promote vitality and balance. In Tantra, practitioners aspire for a harmonious union of physical and spiritual energies through particular breathing exercises and visualization techniques that channel sexual energy upward through the chakras.

Sex magic has the power to strengthen the spiritual bond between partners in relationships. Mutual growth, discovery, and transcendence can occur in a sacred place created by shared intentions and rituals. When two people participate in sex magic together, they discover that the combined experience deepens their spiritual journey as well as their intimate bond. These rituals are collaborative, which supports the notion that sex magic is not only a solo undertaking but can also be a shared one that deepens the link between couples on a spiritual and physical level.

Notwithstanding the wide range of real-world uses of sex magic for spiritual development, it is critical to stress the significance of permission and moral issues in its application. Because sex magic is intimate, it necessitates a high degree of communication and trust between lovers. Practitioners of this holy art must treat one another with dignity and respect, ensuring the experience is mutually beneficial and consensual. Love, respect, and a shared spiritual journey should always be the practice's guiding principles.

In the area of self-discovery and personal empowerment, sex magic has the same transformative power. People have a rare chance to discover and reclaim their sexuality when they purposefully employ their sexual energy. In a world where social taboos and constraints surrounding sexuality are common, sex magic encourages practitioners to accept their impulses without feeling guilty or condemned. This self- acceptance process can foster a more profound sense of self-empowerment and an honest connection with one's desires, which can be a powerful driver for personal progress.

Sex magic can also be included in a more comprehensive spiritual practice, enhancing ritual, meditation, and other contemplative practices. A holistic approach to one's spiritual path is created when sexual practices are purposefully aligned with more general spiritual objectives. Practitioners may discover that the elevated levels of consciousness and energy developed through these practices improve their entire spiritual experiences if they include sex magic in their daily routine.

In summary, there is a wide range of real-world uses for sex magic in spiritual development, including healing, altered states of awareness, manifestation, and self-empowerment. Sex magic, which has its roots in antiquated customs and has been modified for modern settings, acts as a link between the material and the spiritual realms and provides a unique path for personal growth. Practitioners must exercise mindfulness, ethical discernment, and profound reverence for the holiness of this esoteric discipline as they navigate its depths. It takes an open mind, an open heart, and a desire to delve into the deep mysteries of the nexus of spirituality and sexuality to embrace sex magic as a tool for spiritual development.

Ethical considerations in the practice of sex magic

Sex magic is a potent and occult discipline that blends the holy domains of sexuality and spirituality to interact with the personal parts of human life. Ethical issues take center stage in this complex tapestry, directing practitioners toward a thoughtful and responsible interaction with this transformational art. Intentions, consent, and the broader ethical ramifications of engaging in sex magic all need to be carefully considered because of the merging of the material and the metaphysical.

The notion of intentionality is essential to ethical considerations in the field of sex magic. The focused intention that underpins the practice of sex magic is closely linked to its power. Sexual energy is harnessed by practitioners with a specific intention or desire in mind, aiming this powerful force in that direction. As a result, intention clarity becomes essential. To use sex magic ethically, practitioners must carefully consider their reasons and make sure that they are in line with the values of sincerity, harmlessness, and spiritual development. The basis for a responsible and purposeful interaction with the energies called upon in sex magic rituals is this introspective thinking.

The foundation of moral sex magic practice is consent. Practitioners need to emphasize open communication and mutual agreement between all persons involved because of the intimate nature of the profession. This idea applies not only to physical actions but also to the purposes and objectives of the sex magic ritual. All participants must give their informed and enthusiastic agreement before beginning any practice, whether done alone or with a partner. When it comes to shared sex magic experiences, especially when they involve partners, open communication is essential to setting expectations, defining preferences, and reaching a mutual understanding of the objectives. This emphasis strengthens the ethical basis of sex magic on permission, which guarantees that the practice is approached with decency, trust, and dedication to the welfare of all those involved.

Ethical sex magic techniques provide a guiding principle of respect for personal boundaries. Every practitioner possesses a distinct set of personal convictions, comfort zones, and emotional boundaries. In addition to being morally required, respecting these boundaries is also practically essential for the practice's success and wellbeing. In this context, consent encompasses recognizing and accepting personal boundaries, creating a safe and empowering atmosphere for practitioners. Sex magic practitioners who uphold ethics approach the technique with a profound respect for each individual's autonomy and agency, appreciating the singularity of their sexual and spiritual journey.

Sex magic rituals that incorporate deliberate and thoughtful activities strengthen the moral aspects of the art. Drawing on traditions such as Tantra, mindfulness urges practitioners to be attentive to their sensations, emotions, and the energy shared with others while fully present in the moment. This increased consciousness keeps the practice from turning into a purely mechanical or self-serving activity, encouraging ethical considerations and cultivating a conscious relationship with the holy. A profound sense of reverence for the holiness of the act is fostered by mindful involvement with sex magic, which also serves to remind practitioners of the transforming potential inherent in their sexual encounters.

Moreover, ethical sex magic entails a dedication to individual and group welfare. Although sex magic has the potential to be a potent tool for personal growth, moral practitioners understand that all beings are interconnected and that their acts have an effect on the larger community. A responsible approach entails evaluating the possible outcomes of the magical operations, considering the immediate objectives and the fallout on interpersonal relationships, social groups, and the larger cosmic order. Ethical sex magicians strive for balance and harmony, understanding that their goals should enhance the general welfare of themselves and others.

Examining the moral implications of sex magic also highlights the dangers and difficulties that may arise from using the technique. Both physical and energetic imbalances can result from unrestrained or careless use of sexual energy. It is essential for practitioners to be conscious of their shortcomings and weaknesses and to ask for help or mentoring when necessary. Approaching sex magic with a humble acknowledgment of the profound forces at work, ethical practitioners develop a responsible mindset that places self-care and the wellbeing of the greater spiritual community at the forefront.

Understanding and respecting different belief systems is necessary since sex magic is practiced in a variety of cultural and religious situations. Ethical practitioners understand that morality, spirituality, and sexual ethics can have varied meanings within societies and individuals. This acknowledgment supports a variety of viewpoints while maintaining the core values of consent, intentionality, and respect for others. It also fosters an open-minded and inclusive approach to ethical sex magic.

Furthermore, practitioners of sex magic should address their spiritual groups and the outside world with transparency and honesty as part of their ethical obligations. Although sex magic is sometimes associated with privacy and secrecy, ethical practitioners strike a balance by valuing openness and genuineness. To be transparent, one may need to clarify beliefs that could support stigma or judgment, contribute to a larger conversation about spirituality and sexuality, and share insights acquired from the practice. A more knowledgeable and compassionate public viewpoint is fostered by ethical practitioners' candid discussions about the demystification of sex magic.

The moral implications of sex magic change and adapt in light of modern ideals and societal standards, just like any other esoteric practice. The terrain that current practitioners must traverse is molded by changing views on sexual identity, gender relations, and consent. Ethical sex magic recognizes these shifting dynamics and aims to uphold the fundamental values that have steered the practice for centuries while staying in line with growing moral norms.

Finally, when sex magic is practiced responsibly, it becomes a sacred and transforming path that respects the union of spirituality and sexuality. The complex lands of intentionality, consent, boundary respect, mindfulness, and dedication to individual and group wellbeing are navigated by practitioners. Through the observance of these moral guidelines, practitioners of sex magic contribute to a peaceful and enlightened investigation of the divine via the powerful forces of human sexuality. Sex magic's ethical aspects not only aid in the personal development of practitioners but also instill a feeling of accountability and respect for the mighty powers involved in this occult activity.

CHAPTER III

The Energetics of Intimacy

Exploring the energy exchange in intimate relationships

The dynamic flow of energy in intimate relationships—defined by physical and emotional intimacy—goes beyond the apparent and palpable aspects of human connection. The quality and depth of the relationship are shaped by this nuanced interplay between thoughts, emotions, and spiritual forces. One can learn a great deal about the processes that underpin the bonds formed in close relationships by exploring the nuances of this energy exchange.

Emotional energy is central to the energy exchange that occurs in close relationships. Emotions are vital energy that moves between people in a shared dynamic space; they are frequently referred to as the language of the soul. Positive feelings that promote a sense of togetherness and connection, such as love, joy, and compassion, add to the energy exchange's vibrancy and health. On the other hand, negative feelings like fear, resentment, or rage can cause discord and upset the equilibrium of energy in a partnership. Fostering a solid and durable relationship between couples depends on emotional energy awareness and conscious management.

In addition, people's intentions and thoughts play a big part in the energy exchange in close relationships. Concentrating ideas toward beneficial and constructive

consequences is the source of intentionality's strength. The energetic synergy between couples is enhanced when there is unity regarding goals, aspirations, or ideals for their relationship. On the other hand, discordant intents or covert goals could cause misunderstandings or a sense of detachment from the energy exchange. Open and transparent communication becomes essential to ensure a healthy energy exchange, build trust, and align intentions.

Intimate relationships require spiritual energy, frequently linked to a stronger feeling of purpose and inner self-connection. A strong sense of oneness and purpose can be created between lovers when their spiritual energies coincide. This spiritual resonance might be a commitment to one another's and our personal and collective progress or similar ideals or beliefs. To create a holy place for mutual progress, partners who work on their spiritual connection may discover that their relationship is a source of inspiration, understanding, and a shared sense of the transcendent.

Intimate connections have a physical component, a concrete manifestation of the energy exchange that carries spiritual, mental, and emotional energies. Energy moves between partners through physical contact, loving gestures, and sexual intimacy. In addition to providing pleasure, the material energy exchange helps to strengthen the emotional and spiritual connection. The general energy exchange is improved by deliberate and thoughtful physical interactions, fostering closeness, safety, and emotional well-being in the partnership.

Understanding the idea of energetic boundaries is essential to investigating the energy exchange in close relationships. Every person has their energetic signature shaped by their spiritual beliefs, feelings, and experiences. It is necessary to uphold these energetic boundaries to preserve a harmonious and balanced energy exchange. Mutual respect and emotional safety are fostered by partners aware of each other's energetic demands and boundaries. Being mindful of one's limits

promotes a more genuine and peaceful energy exchange by averting inadvertent energy leakage or invasion from one partner to another.

Intimate connections involve an energy exchange that naturally incorporates the idea of reciprocity. Energy exchanges that are reciprocal establish a dynamic balance in the partnership. Energy flows freely between partners who exhibit a healthy give-and-take dynamic, thereby preserving and enhancing their relationship. This interchange includes understanding, spiritual uplift, emotional support, and money or practical transactions. When reciprocity is practiced in a relationship, both parties support each other's energetic health, promoting shared accountability and mutual development.

An imbalance in the energy flow between partners might lead to difficulties in the energy exchange. One spouse always giving more than getting might be a sign of this imbalance and can cause feelings of exhaustion or anger. On the other hand, a partnership may develop an unhealthy dependency if one person is overly dependent on their energies. It takes open communication, self-awareness, and a desire to examine and modify the relationship's energetic dynamics to identify and correct these imbalances. A relationship's general well-being and durability are enhanced by partners who take an active role in reestablishing equilibrium in the energy exchange.

Cultural and socioeconomic factors can also impact intimate connection energy exchange. Cultural norms, gender roles, and societal expectations can influence people's expression and reception of energy in relationships. To traverse the intricacies of cultural expectations and cultivate an authentic and conscious energy exchange, partners must be aware of these external influences. Partners can redefine and explore the energy dynamics in a way consistent with their beliefs and goals when they embrace a shared understanding of the cultural environment.

Examining the energy exchange in close relationships necessitates approaching the processes at work with awareness and consciousness. Self-awareness- enhancing activities like mindfulness, meditation, and reflective journaling can help people become more aware of their energy and how it affects their relationships. When partners participate in these activities together, they may discover that their connection becomes more profound due to their shared reflective moments, enhancing and promoting a more prosperous and conscious energy exchange.

The energy flow in close relationships involves a multifaceted interaction between mental, emotional, and spiritual powers. Fostering a strong, harmonious, and satisfying relationship requires awareness of and deliberate control over this energy exchange. Collaboratively, partners who skillfully handle the various domains of emotional, mental, spiritual, and physical energy help shape a robust, dynamic relationship that aligns with the transformational power of human connection. Intimate partners can create a space where love, understanding, and spiritual resonance flourish by investigating and fostering the energy exchange. This lays the groundwork for enduring and meaningful interactions.

Techniques for enhancing energetic connection

The web of human connection is not limited to what is apparent; it is also woven with subtle energies that influence the nature and depth of connections. Developing an energetic connection with people is more than just talking to them or doing things together; it's about sensing the minute currents of energy that move back and forth between people. Stronger and more meaningful shared experiences can result from the capacity to improve and expand energetic connections, whether in personal relationships, friendships, or professional partnerships. This paper investigates ways to enhance active connection and offers insights into methods that promote a greater sense of cohesion, empathy, and understanding.

Based on ancient contemplative traditions, mindfulness is a primary method for improving energetic connection. Cultivating mindfulness entails developing a keen awareness of one's thoughts, feelings, and sensations in the current moment. When mindfulness is used in interpersonal situations, people can tune into the subtleties of the energetic exchange and be truly present with others. Acknowledging the other person's active presence while paying complete attention to the speaker without passing judgment or being distracted is known as mindful listening, and it promotes a deeper level of connection. Self-awareness is a component of mindfulness as well since it teaches people how to identify and control their energy states, facilitating more genuine and purposeful communication.

Using the breath as a vital life force, breathwork is a potent practice to enhance energetic connection. Intentional and conscious breathing not only helps people relax and find their rhythm, but it also produces a harmonious, energetic resonance. By aligning their energy to a shared rhythm, practices like synchronized breathing, which involves people coordinating their breath, enhance the sense of connectedness. Additionally, breathwork exercises open the body's energetic channels, facilitating a more open-minded energy exchange between people. Conscious breathing is a bridge that connects people energetically, whether they practice it alone or with others. It creates a shared sense of presence and connection.

With its many forms and methods, meditation provides a significant way to improve energetic connection. Through meditation, one can develop a condition of inner calm and presence that opens the door to a higher level of consciousness under the surface of ordinary cognition. Couples or groups who meditate together may feel a stronger feeling of shared energy in the context of relationships. Meditation techniques that emphasize developing loving-kindness or compassion create a broad, energetic connection, promoting connectivity with all living things. Through meditation, people learn to still their minds and open their hearts, which opens up the active space between them and allows for a deeper, more genuine connection.

Through the expressive movement of the body, movement disciplines like Tai Chi and dance offer dynamic options for improving energy connection. Particularly with dance, people may connect and communicate without using words on an intense level. When two people dance together, for example, they exchange energy by imitating and reacting to one another's actions. Dancing together creates a shared physique that serves as a medium for energy flow, strengthening bonds beyond spoken words. Similarly, the ancient Chinese martial art of Tai Chi strongly emphasizes deliberate, slow movements that foster a heightened awareness of the body's energy. When these movement-based methods are combined, they strengthen the energy bond by promoting a common language of fluidity and expression.

Due to their energy qualities, many cultures and spiritual traditions have held crystals and gemstones in high regard. Choosing stones in tune with particular traits or aims is essential when using crystals in energetic connection techniques. Individuals or partners can hold or place crystals in a shared space, enabling the stones' energy qualities to improve the atmosphere. Rose quartz, a love and compassion-related crystal, can be utilized to strengthen the energetic bond in partnerships. The deliberate usage of crystals is consistent with the idea that these gems from Earth can magnify and harmonize energy, promoting a more balanced and sensitive connection between people.

Chanting, singing bowls, and toning are examples of sound therapy, a vibrational method to improve energetic connection. Sound has a specific frequency that reverberates with the body's active centers, altering the body's entire energy field profoundly. When two people chant or tone simultaneously, their voice vibrations coordinate and produce a shared resonance that transcends aural perception. Because of their melodic tones, singing bowls are also used to harmonize and balance the body's energy centers. Through the shared experience of sound therapy, the vibrating essence of unity and connection is tapped into, transcending verbal communication.

The development of empathy is one psychological strategy that has a significant impact on people's energy connection to one another. The capacity for empathy is sharing and comprehending the emotions of another, building an emotional and energetic connection between people. The sensation of connection is strengthened by engaging in empathic listening, which involves tuning into the emotions and active signals conveyed and hearing what is said. Through empathy, people can tune into each other's energy levels and develop a mutual understanding beyond spoken words. People help create a more sympathetic and energetically resonant relationship by acknowledging and accepting the emotional and energetic experiences of others.

Yoga is an age-old Indian discipline that comprehensively integrates movement, breath, and mindfulness to improve energetic connection. Specifically, partner yoga involves people moving and posing in unison to create a shared sense of harmony and balance. The deliberate synchronization of movement and breathing balances the energy flow in both people, fostering a sense of oneness. Whether practiced alone or with a partner, yoga strengthens the energetic bond by encouraging a state of presence, self-awareness, and alignment with the subtle energies that permeate the body and the space between people.

Adding rituals to everyday life or shared experiences is one way to improve the energetic connection in relationships. Simple or complex, rituals establish a framework that recognizes the holiness of events and connections. Shared rituals can include lighting candles together, giving thanks, or doing symbolic actions that have special meaning for each individual. These deliberate actions act as energetic anchors, promoting a feeling of oneness and connection while rising above the ordinary and giving ordinary events more prosperous and meaningful energy.

Exploring outdoors together can improve energy connection by connecting with the reviving and balancing energies of the natural world. Activities that involve hiking, camping, or just spending time in nature with a partner or group produce a shared experience that is in tune with the cycles of the Earth. Because of its innate vigor and energy, nature is a catalyst to balance and ground people's energies. People attuned to the tranquility and brightness of the outdoors find a more profound sense of connection against the backdrop of natural environments' simplicity and beauty.

Ultimately, visualization becomes a powerful tool for improving energetic connection by utilizing the mind's ability to generate shared, vibrant experiences. Individuals or partners can picture energetic cords linking their hearts or a shared active space between them in guided visualizations. By utilizing visualization techniques, people can access their minds' creative and manifesting potential, which helps them co-create a more elevated, energetic connection. The knowledge that the mind is fundamental in forming and affecting the energy dynamics in relationships is consistent with the purposeful use of visualization.

To sum up, the methods for improving energy connection include a wide range of approaches that involve the body, mind, and spirit. These methods, which can have their roots in antiquated customs or originate from modern methodologies, provide people and partners with opportunities to enhance their sense of harmony, comprehension, and mutual resonance.

The study of energetic connection reaches beyond language barriers and into the nuanced domains that influence the fabric of interpersonal interactions. By incorporating these approaches into one's daily routine and communal experiences, people can foster a deeper and more fulfilling bond that surpasses the apparent aspects of interpersonal relationships.

Balancing personal and shared energies

People walk a fine line between their shared and personal energy in the complex dance of relationships. Everyone possesses an energetic signature shaped by their life experiences, feelings, and spiritual preferences. Although the foundation of connection is the entwining of human energy, a harmonious equilibrium that respects individuality and shared experiences is also necessary to sustain a good relationship. This essay delves into the intricacies of coexisting and the skill of fostering a connection that permits both mutual thriving and personal progress. It also examines the dynamics of balancing private and shared energies within relationships.

Boundaries are fundamental to the interaction of shared and personal energies. An essential part of preserving personal integrity in a partnership is setting and honoring limits. Personal limits define the room and freedom each person needs to be themselves, seek personal development, and care for themselves. A peaceful interchange of energies is fostered by partners who intentionally communicate and respect each other's boundaries. This shared knowledge makes it possible for people to cohabit with their autonomy and blend their energy in a way that promotes their relationship and personal well-being.

In a partnership, effective communication is essential for navigating the complexities of shared and personal energies. People can communicate their needs, wants, and worries through open and honest conversation, which promotes comprehension of each other's energetic states. Open lines of communication between partners make it possible to identify and correct any potential imbalances in the energy exchange. People contribute to a partnership where shared and personal energies are acknowledged by sharing their experiences and expectations.

Consisting self-awareness is essential to balance one's own and community energies. Self-aware people grow to know their requirements, triggers, and energetic states. This knowledge makes it possible for people to manage their energies mindfully, which promotes more purposeful and mindful interactions with their relationships. Self-awareness also entails understanding how other people's energies affect one's own, enabling people to distinguish between demands from their true selves. Prioritizing self-awareness allows partners to understand each other better, which fosters a peaceful environment where shared and personal energies come together.

Accepting the reciprocity principle helps relationships balance shared and individual energies. Giving and receiving, in return, creates a dynamic interchange that keeps the relationship going while enabling people to meet their own needs. Actively supporting, caring for, and understanding one another makes a space that nurtures individual and shared energies. This principle emphasizes that the well-being of one person is closely linked to the well-being of the partnership as a whole, acknowledging the innate interdependence within relationships.

Understanding "we" and "me" time becomes essential to balance individual and group energies. When partners consciously set aside time for hobbies, personal interests, or introspection, they make room for personal development and renewal. In addition, quality time and shared activities foster the development of a shared energy field that fortifies the relationship between partners. A thoughtful strategy that acknowledges the value of individual autonomy and communal connection is needed to balance personal and shared time. The dynamic interaction of shared and private energies nourishes relationships that respect one another's need for alone and togetherness.

The capacity for empathy, or the understanding and sharing of another person's emotions, becomes essential for striking a balance between one's own and other people's energies. Empathic partners are sensitive to each other's emotional moods and help one another better grasp the subtle energetic dynamics in a relationship. With empathy, people can sensitively and compassionately manage the ups and downs of their own and other people's energy. Partners contribute to a relationship where personal and shared energies are acknowledged and cherished by recognizing and supporting one another's experiences.

Making thoughtful decisions in a relationship means considering how decisions affect shared and personal energies. Harmonious cohabitation of energies is facilitated by partners who approach decisions with a collective understanding of their individual and the relationship's demands. This thoughtful approach encompasses essential life decisions, everyday activities, and shared duties, enabling a common vision that aligns with each person's unique goals. Making decisions with awareness opens the door to deliberate co-creation and promotes a dynamic balance of shared and personal energies in relationships.

Developing a common goal or vision for the partnership is a unifying factor, aligning shared and personal energy. Couples with similar beliefs, aspirations, or objectives for the future establish a framework that directs the flow of energy in their relationship. This common goal is a source of motivation, giving the relationship direction and significance. While personal development is still significant, having a common goal enables people to focus on something more meaningful that benefits the relationship as a whole.

The balancing work of personal and shared energies

gains depth via spiritual alignment, whether inside a standard belief system or via mutual respect's spiritual journey. A sacred atmosphere is created when partners who pursue spirituality or encourage each other's separate spiritual endeavors blend personal and shared energies. A shared spiritual foundation enables people to negotiate life's problems together, and spiritual alignment becomes a guiding force that imbues the partnership with a sense of oneness and sublime connection.

Resolving conflicts becomes crucial to preserving the

balance of one's own and other people's energies. Relationship conflicts frequently result from disparities in viewpoints, wants, or energetic levels. Conflicts can become opportunities for growth rather than causes of depletion in a relationship when partners approach them with empathy, openness, and a commitment to resolution. To resolve conflicts effectively, parties must be prepared to make concessions that respect their respective and shared needs, validate their experiences, and actively listen to one another. Couples can maintain a robust and adaptable energetic balance in their relationship by managing disagreements with mindfulness.

Recognizing and accepting change facilitates the

continuous balancing of shared and personal energies in a relationship. Like people, relationships naturally go through stages of development, change, and evolution. Couples who accept that change is inevitable acknowledge that their individual and joint energy may fluctuate. This recognition enables people to deal with change flexibly and adaptively, keeping the connection dynamic and sensitive to the changing requirements of both parties. Partners add to a relationship by developing an acceptance of the mobility of their individual and joint energy.

That endures the changing seasons of life while remaining robust and vibrant.

In summary, maintaining a healthy balance between

one's own and the relationship's shared energy is a complex dance that calls for self-awareness, communication, and intentionality. When partners successfully maintain this delicate balance, they create an environment where mutual prospering and personal development can live peacefully. A durable relationship, transforming and tuned into the subtle dance of human connection, is fostered by the dynamic force created by the interplay of shared and personal energy. People can co-create an active and satisfying relationship that honors the individual contributions of each partner while fostering the union's collective energy when they learn to respect both their authenticity and the shared energy in the relationship.

CHAPTER IV

Rituals for Sacred Connection

Designing and performing sacred rituals for couples

The transformational power of love, emotional connection, and shared experiences are the threads that weave close relationships together. The planning and executing of sacred rituals for couples becomes a powerful instrument for strengthening bonds, encouraging spiritual closeness, and developing a sense of shared purpose within this complex web. Whether created by hand or rooted in old customs, sacred rituals offer a holy setting where couples can delve into their love and infuse it with the divine feeling. This essay delves into the meaning, components, and transforming potential of these deliberate and shared activities, examining the art of creating and executing holy rituals for couples.

Understanding the sacred in everyday life is

fundamental to creating meaningful rituals for a marriage. Rather than being ornate or ostentatious, religious rituals get their significance from the shared meaning, presence, and intention permeating the actions carried out. Couples can start by listing the meaningful components of their everyday life, such as a morning ritual, dinners together, or quiet times for introspection. By using intentionality and attentive presence, these commonplace acts can become the blank canvas on which sacred rituals are created, converting the ordinary into the holy.

Sacred ritual design is a cooperative investigation of meaning, symbolism, and shared principles. Couples can have candid discussions about their spiritual views, goals, and the symbols that are meaningful to them personally. These conversations set the stage for co- creating rituals that speak to the couple's spiritual path. Collaboratively designing the rituals using inspiration from nature, cultural traditions, or personal symbols guarantees that the rituals accurately capture the spirit of the relationship.

The intimacy of a shared house or the vastness of the outdoors might serve as the hallowed place for rituals. Establishing a physical or symbolic area for sacred rituals creates a barrier separating these deliberate times from the regular course of daily existence. For the pair, this area acts as a haven, encouraging awareness, concentration, and respect for the sanctity of their relationship. You can add significance and intention to the environment by lighting candles, placing sentimental items, or selecting a particular spot outside.

Adding sensory experiences, establishing intentions, and incorporating symbolism are some components of holy rituals for couples. Symbolism offers a vocabulary for partners to express their shared beliefs and deeper meanings. Whether by employing specific colors, symbolic items, or customs derived from cultural customs, symbolism deepens the meaning of the shared experience. Establishing an intention entails making a conscious decision about the ritual's goal: to show gratitude, strengthen emotional ties, or begin a common spiritual path. Setting specific aims helps the ritual's transforming potential and balances the couple's energies. Incorporating many senses through sensory experiences, such as smells, sounds, or tactile components, strengthens the couple's connection to the present and amplifies the ritual's overall effect.

The practice of conscious presence is one of the most potent components of sacred ceremonies for couples. Being mindful entails giving your entire attention to the here and now while maintaining an impartial and open mind. By deliberately slowing down, concentrating on their breathing, and fully engaging their senses, couples can incorporate mindfulness into their routines. Couples are better able to connect deeply and fully to each other and to the divine nature of the shared moment when there is a mindful presence.

Sacred rituals are frequently performed through shared activities, symbolic gestures, and ritualistic behaviors. These deeds intentionally represent the couple's commitment to one another and their shared spiritual path, or embodied prayer. Candle lighting, vows or significant words exchanged, or the formation of a holy circle are ritualistic acts. Ritualistic repeating of these acts generates a rhythm that enhances the shared experience's energy resonance, taking it from the commonplace into the sacred.

Sacred rituals are a habit that couples carry into their relationship regularly, transcending special events. Incorporating these deliberate acts into daily routines fosters a continuous sense of spiritual connectedness and ordinary meaning. Couples can create routines that include nighttime, morning, or weekly rituals to provide stability for their spiritual path together. Maintaining the spiritual underpinning of the partnership and creating a sense of continuity are fostered by regular participation in religious rituals.

Examining shared values and ideas is sometimes a part of sacred ceremonies for couples. Couples can partake in shared spiritual activities like meditation, prayer, or reading philosophical materials to comprehend one another's spiritual viewpoints better. Through this joint investigation, partners can grow from one another, share ideas, and co-create a spiritual language that strengthens their bond. Accepting each other's differences in spirituality creates a climate in which each spouse feels heard, valued, and encouraged on their unique path.

Sacred rituals can transform lives by enabling transcendent moments that strengthen a bond that endures despite life's ups and downs. This is especially true for couples. These customs act as touchstones, reminding the couple of the holy bond that unites them and anchoring them to the deeper levels of their relationship. Sacred rites enhance happy occasions by adding a feeling of the divine to the festivities. During challenging times, the couple can traverse obstacles with grit and support from each other in a sacred space provided by these rituals, which become sources of strength and comfort.

When couples include holy rituals in their relationship, it creates a familiar story that goes beyond the separate narratives of each partner. To commemorate essential occasions like anniversaries, joint achievements, or times of personal and interpersonal development, couples can establish rituals. These customs become chapters in the couple's standard narrative, combining their unique stories into a tapestry of mutual love, spiritual growth, and shared experiences.

Couples can also receive spiritual nutrition via sacred rituals, which refuel their relationship's emotional and physical reserves. Intentional pauses that facilitate introspection, connection, and the infusion of spiritual energy benefit relationships, just as people need time for rest and renewal for their overall health. To maintain the vitality of their relationship, couples can create rituals explicitly centered around renewal and restoration. This will establish a consistent rhythm of spiritual feeding.

Sacred rituals for couples affect the energetic environment surrounding them and the relationship itself. The couple's deliberate and spiritual actions create an energy field that involves the places they live in and the people they come into contact with. This uplifting and holy energy adds to the larger fabric of human connection by bringing love, oneness, and the transforming power of purposeful interactions into collective awareness.

To sum up, creating and carrying out holy rituals for couples is a meaningful and purposeful practice that enhances the spiritual aspects of close relationships. These deliberate activities strengthen the bond between spouses and give their relationship a sense of the sacred, from co-creating significant symbols to the thoughtful execution of ritualistic acts. Couples can express their love, dedication, and shared journey via holy rituals, which create their own language. These transcendent moments take a couple's relationship beyond the ordinary and into the divine. Couples who make and carry out sacred rituals learn about the transforming power that comes from purposefully incorporating the holy into their shared life.

Incorporating meditation and visualization into intimate practices

The confluence of spirituality and intimacy is a significant chance for partners to strengthen their bond, cultivate understanding, and delve into the sacred aspects of their partnership. Visualization and meditation are particularly effective instruments among the many techniques that connect the spiritual and personal spheres. These practices, which have their roots in contemporary contemplative traditions and ancient wisdom, provide a means for couples to create a shared space where their minds, bodies, and spirits come together and improve the physical aspects of their relationship. This paper investigates the incorporation of meditation and visualization into personal practices, examining the importance, advantages, and methods that enhance the relationship's shared and personalized aspects.

With roots firmly planted in many different spiritual traditions, meditation is fundamental for people looking for inner peace, awareness of themselves, and a sense of presence. Meditation becomes an effective technique for developing heightened awareness and connection between partners when included in intimate activities. To start, couples can do joint meditation sessions, setting aside time and space for each other's reflection. Partners can direct their attention to the present moment by focusing on their breath while seated comfortably. A familiar cadence is created between the repetitive inhalation and exhalation, aligning their energies and encouraging synchronization.

One of the core components of meditation, mindful breathing, is especially important for personal practices. In addition to bringing couples into the present, conscious breathing bridges their relationship's energy and physical aspects. Synchronized breathing exercises can help couples create a familiar rhythm by intentionally aligning their breaths. As partners become more attuned to each other's physical presence and the subtle energetic exchanges that take place with every breath, this deliberate act deepens their sense of connection.

A key element of meditation is the practice of mindfulness, which is developing an accepting and nonjudgmental awareness of the present moment. Mindfulness encourages partners to focus entirely on the feelings, details, and sensations of their shared experience when engaging in intimate practices. With mindfulness, couples may enjoy the richness of the present without letting worries about the past or the future interfere, whether they are having physical intimacy, eating together, or just being physically present for one another. Couples give each other this elevated sense of presence as a gift, laying the groundwork for a more intimate and profound bond.

Formal sitting sessions are just one aspect of meditation techniques; other approaches involve movement, the senses, and the body. Yoga allows couples to investigate the relationship between shared presence, breath awareness, and physical flexibility. It is frequently referred to as a moving meditation. Specifically created for couples, partner yoga incorporates coordinated poses and movements that foster mutual support, trust, and balance. Practicing these alignment techniques can make an energetic resonance that improves one's sense of total connectedness and physical alignment.

Couples can also investigate the incorporation of meditation into their practices by engaging in guided meditation sessions. During meditation sessions, partners can alternately lead each other, emphasizing relaxation, emotional connection, or shared aims. Couples can explore the spiritual aspects of their relationship and the landscapes of their emotions and wants by going on guided inner excursions during these sessions. Whether with audio direction or recorded guided meditations, this joint investigation strengthens the bond between the two people.

Visualization entails conjuring up images in the mind that represent particular feelings, events, or sensations as an adjunct to meditation. Visualization becomes a tool for co-creating shared mental landscapes that deepen relationships when integrated into intimate practices. Engaging in guided visualization exercises can help couples visualize a shared place that is a haven of love, peace, and understanding. Partners have a sense of purpose and shared vision as they immerse themselves in this shared mental environment, with the visualization acting as a bridge to connect their inner worlds.

In addition to exploring one another's goals and wants, shared visualizations involve co-creating future experiences. In joint vision exercises, partners can visualize their hopes, goals, and relationship development in their minds. This cooperative gesture strengthens the bond between them and acts as a potent catalyst for bringing their intents and energies into harmony. The couple's shared visions guide their path, fostering a sense of purpose and understanding between them.

Examining sensory awareness is another aspect of integrating meditation and visualization into personal practices. Couples can tune into the subtleties of their shared experiences through meditation, cultivating a heightened feeling of presence. By approaching each sensory experience with focused awareness, a couple can delve further into their relationship, whether it is through taste, smell, touch, or sound. For instance, mindful touch entails sharing intimate physical contact while paying close attention to the energies, textures, and sensations shared between partners. Engaging in sensory awareness invites partners to be present with one another on a sensory level, which enhances intimacy.

One of the main components of meditation, breath awareness, serves as a guide to help one navigate the ups and downs of intimate experiences. When they are physically close, partners can practice breath-focused techniques that coordinate their inhalations and exhalations. This breathing exercise improves the physical aspects of intimacy and fosters a deep sense of energetic connection. Breath alignment becomes a subtle yet potent instrument for facilitating a coordinated and harmonic connection by attuning to each other's energies.

Beyond the immediate experiences, the relationship's general well-being is enhanced by integrating meditation and visualization into intimate practices. Couples can manage stress, build resilience, and navigate the difficulties of everyday life with the help of these strategies. Partners can use mindfulness developed via meditation as a resource during trying times, providing a haven of clarity and quiet amidst life's ups and downs. Couples can use visualization as a creative outlet to envision solutions, goals they have in common, and how their relationship will always grow.

Emotional intimacy can also be attained through incorporating visualization and meditation into personal rituals. Partners can feel seen, heard, and fully understood in this place because of the increased awareness and presence fostered by these activities. Couples can embrace vulnerability and honesty through meditation, which strongly emphasizes nonjudgmental awareness. This creates an atmosphere where feelings can be acknowledged and accepted without fear of rejection or shame. Couples can explore the landscapes of their emotions, wants, and the unsaid aspects of their relationship by using visualization as a shared language.

Deepening the spiritual aspects of the relationship is where meditation and visualization in intimate practices can have a transforming effect. Engaging in these techniques invites couples to explore their inner worlds and enter hallowed realms of self-discovery and mutual exploration. The joint breathwork exercises, guided visualizations, and group meditation sessions establish a common language beyond spoken words, enabling couples to communicate on a level that transcends the material world and touches the spiritual realms.

Intimate practices that incorporate meditation and visualization support the co-creation of a physically and spiritually rewarding relationship. Through intention, presence, and a feeling of the sacred, these activities become the threads that weave the relationship's tapestry. Engaging in peaceful meditation, practicing joint visualizations, or incorporating mindfulness into intimate times, couples that take this path learn how deeply the mind, body, and spirit are intertwined within the sacred space of their partnership.

Creating a sacred space for spiritual connection

The search for spiritual connection frequently finds resonance in the intimate spaces we share with our partners, transcending the bounds of the outside world in the fabric of human connections. Establishing a sacred space within the personal sphere—a room, a shared residence, or a symbolic shrine, for example—becomes a meaningful activity for couples looking to strengthen their spiritual ties. This essay dissects the layers of meaning and intention that come together to form a sanctuary where the divine and the personal intersect, and it does so by examining the significance, components, and transformative potential of creating a sacred space for spiritual connection within the context of intimate relationships.

The notion of a holy place has its origins in various spiritual traditions. It reflects the universal human tendency to set aside symbolic or physical locations for spiritual connection with the divine. Establishing a holy place in close relationships is a conscious endeavor, a co-creation between partners who want to bring a feeling of the sacred into their shared times. This action entails more than just setting up the room's physical components; it also entails giving it purpose, significance, and an awareness of a relationship beyond the mundane.

A holy place in a relationship can take on many different shapes depending on the partners' particular inclinations, values, and dynamics. It could appear to some as a unique space decorated with holy objects, spiritual symbols, and dim lighting. For others, it could be a little altar or a gathering of sentimental objects in a corner of a common area. The room itself isn't important; what matters is the couple's intentionality in designating it as sacred, using it as a canvas to paint the colors of their shared spiritual journey.

Intentionality is a critical component in creating a sacred space; it is the deliberate decision to mark a particular location or time as religious. This intentionality is a mutual agreement between couples, denoting a pledge to bring a sense of reverence and spiritual connection into their shared experiences. It is a knowledge that everything changes in this place—the commonplace becomes exceptional, and the sacred becomes earthly. Couples who practice intentionality together set a path to co-create a holy story for their relationship, revealed through frequent rituals, significant symbols, and purposeful moments of intimacy.

To create a sacred place, rituals are essential. They provide a deliberate and regulated means of spiritual connection for couples. Simple rituals like sharing a candle, meditating together, or expressing gratitude for life's blessings might serve as examples of these. These rituals are repeated, creating a rhythm that ties the couple to the spiritual side of their relationship. Using ritual, partners establish a common vocabulary of the sacred and harness the transforming potential of repetition, which enhances the sacred space's energetic resonance.

Incorporating significant symbols into the sacred space allows couples to express the breadth of their spiritual bond. These icons could be derived from similar ideals, cultural origins, or personal convictions. These symbols, religious icons, symbolic objects, or representations of a common goal act as pillars that firmly establish the couple in their shared spiritual story. Symbols in the sacred area evoke a sense of continuity and connection and manifest the couple's dedication to their spiritual path

Sacred items further enhance the religious manifestation in the shared space. Some artifacts, including gemstones, holy books, or souvenirs gathered during significant travels, could have spiritual or personal meaning. Every item serves as a container for the goals, memories, and energy that couples exchange. The couple's spiritual essence resonates with the tactile and visual landscape created by the deliberate arrangement of these artifacts within the sacred area. The area becomes a living testament to the typical path of development, change, and spiritual connection when holy artifacts are present.

An important factor in determining the atmosphere of a sacred site is lighting. Soft, warm lighting creates an ambiance of peace and reflection, which invites couples to enter a shared area of reflection. Candles have a long-standing symbolic meaning of enlightenment and spiritual awakening. As a practice in and of itself, lighting candles together denotes the desire to bring light into the relationship, chase out darkness, and promote a sense of spiritual clarity. The dance of lighting creates a shared illumination tapestry, serving as a metaphor for the dance of energies within the sacred place.

Soundscapes enhance the sacred environment's auditory aspects, whether created by music, chanting, or natural noises. Couples might select sounds that inspire calm and tranquility or correspond with their spiritual preferences. The deliberate use of sound in the hallowed area produces a visceral experience that strengthens the bond between spouses and the space's spiritual nature. The couple's shared auditory language, which speaks to the soul directly and beyond words, is expressed through selecting particular sounds.

By using natural elements, the sacred space creates a bridge between the outside and internal worlds. The additions of potted plants, crystals, or miniature versions of natural elements infuse the compact area with the vibrancy of nature. Nature's innate ability to inspire feelings of wonder, beauty, and connectivity is similar to how spiritual aspects of interpersonal relationships are reflected in it. Couples can create a harmonic balance between the ethereal and the earthly by including nature components into their sacred space, thereby inviting the grounding and renewing energies of the natural world.

It takes more than just physical components to create a sacred space for spiritual connection; it also entails cultivating a shared presence and conscious awareness inside the area. Couples might enter a condition of shared quiet and receptivity by doing contemplative activities or meditation together. As partners grow attuned to the subtle energies and nuances within themselves and the shared space, the deliberate focus on the present moment opens a portal to the divine. Being mindfully present in the sacred space strengthens the bond between spouses and creates an avenue for communion that reaches into the depths of the soul.

A holy space has the power to transform because it can act as a haven, a place where a couple can go to escape the pressures of the outside world and connect with the core of their everyday spirituality. This retreat becomes a haven for reflection, recovery, and developing a shared future vision. As a daily routine or in times of celebration or adversity, partners can go to the sacred space to rekindle the spiritual spark that keeps them connected.

Establishing and preserving a sacred space in a partnership requires constant focus, intentionality, and cooperation. It is a dynamic painting that changes with

The spiritual journey of the partners. The sacred space serves as a touchstone for couples navigating life's challenges and a reminder of the richness, beauty, and spiritual potential innate in their relationship. The hallowed area becomes a living example of their common faith and a symbol of deliberate love's tenacity and transforming force.

In conclusion, creating a sacred place for spiritual connection within an intimate relationship takes a deep and deliberate practice. It entails building a sanctuary together that is intentional, meaningful, and filled with shared rituals. Every element—from lighting, sound, and natural elements to incorporating significant symbols and artifacts—contributes to the shared space's embodiment of the sacred. Couples can experience a journey beyond the ordinary and unlock the transformational potential of shared spirituality by purposefully cultivating a holy narrative. Their spiritual bond flourishes in the sanctuary they co-create inside the fabric of their relationship, and the sacred space becomes a living monument to that connection's breadth, beauty, and enduring nature.

CHAPTER V

Tantra and the Art of Mindful Lovemaking

Understanding the principles of Tantra

Tantra, which originates in ancient India's spiritual traditions, is well-known and of great interest in modern times due to its all-encompassing perspective on spirituality, personal growth, and close relationships. Tantra is frequently misinterpreted and misunderstood, and it's more than just sexual visuals and exotic rituals. Fundamentally, Tantra is an elaborate spiritual doctrine that recognizes the interdependence of energy, awareness, and all facets of existence. This essay examines the core ideas of Tantra, illuminating its spiritual core, methods, and possibilities for transforming individuals and interpersonal relationships.

Tantra's fundamental tenet is the acknowledgment of the divine in all facets of existence. Tantra sees the material world as a manifestation of the holy rather than something that stands in the way of spiritual development. This viewpoint holds that the physical world, emotions, and the body are sacred and deserve investigation to achieve spiritual enlightenment. Tantra invites people to connect with life actively, realizing the innate divinity present in every moment, experience, and form instead of attempting to transcend the material world.

The idea of Shakti and Shiva, or the dynamic interaction of feminine and male energy, is fundamental to Tantric philosophy. Shiva embodies the awareness, calm, and aggressive power frequently associated with the masculine. At the same time, Shakti represents the creative, nurturing, and receptive force, which is often linked with the feminine. Tantric rituals recognize the innate balance and complementarity of the feminine and male components of existence and work to integrate and combine these energies within an individual. This union accepts the dual nature of every individual and is not limited to gender roles.

The practice of awareness and mindfulness cultivation is highly valued in Tantra. Tantra's techniques encourage people to live fully in the present and give conscious attention to every experience. In Tantra, mindfulness entails an impartial awareness of one's body, breath, sensations, and emotions. This enhanced consciousness permeates all facets of life and is not restricted to meditation techniques. It cultivates a profound sense of connectedness to unfolding every moment, present, and thankfulness.

Tantra's emphasis on sexuality is fundamental, yet it's sometimes misunderstood as the central theme. Tantric philosophy views sexuality as a potent and sacred force that can be used to achieve spiritual development and transformation. The goal of sexual energy-based tantric rituals is to transcend sensual pleasure and establish a connection with the holy. These exercises strongly emphasize awareness of partner energy exchange, deep presence, and mindfulness. In Tantra, engaging in sexual intimacy can lead to spiritual communion, wherein one seeks a transcendent unity, and the boundaries between oneself and the other disappear.

The idea of Kundalini is another essential Tantric element. Kundalini, the symbol of latent spiritual force, is frequently shown as a coiling serpent at the base of the spine. This energy is channeled through the chakras, or energy centers, along the spine through Tantric rituals. A stronger bond with the divine, elevated states of awareness, and spiritual awakening are all linked to Kundalini activation. Tantric practitioners use specialized techniques, including breathing exercises, meditation, and visualization, to help Kundalini energy awaken gradually and safely.

Tantra also highlights the significance of ceremonies and rituals to establish a connection with the sacred. These rites, which employ mantras, offerings, and holy symbols, can be complex or straightforward. Tantric rituals build a spiritual connection, call in divine energies, and create a sacred place. Whether carried out alone or with others, these rituals offer a means of connecting with life's more spiritual aspects and rising above the mundane.

While sacred sexuality is central to Tantric practice, it is essential to emphasize that Tantra does not condone promiscuity or hedonism. Tantric sexuality, on the other hand, is based on the values of spiritual connection, mindfulness, and respect. Partners are urged to approach each other with reverence and a keen awareness of the energetic exchange occurring, focusing on conscious and intentional lovemaking. Tantric sexuality seeks to create a connection that goes beyond the individual and serves as a doorway to spiritual unification by going beyond simple physical pleasure.

Tantra acknowledges the significance of the human body as a medium for spiritual communication. Tantric traditions frequently use yoga, breathwork, and physical exercise to cultivate a vibrant and healthy body. Taking care of one's body is regarded as a spiritual activity since it is believed to be a sacred temple containing the divine essence. Tantric practitioners aim to achieve mental, bodily, and spiritual balance through mindful movement, breath awareness, and intentional involvement with the body.

The guru-disciple dynamic, or the teacher-student relationship, is a significant feature of Tantra. In Tantric traditions, trainees are supposed to be guided on the spiritual path by a certified teacher called a guru. As a mentor, the guru helps students grow spiritually by sharing knowledge, offering advice, and encouraging their progress. A guru and disciple's relationship is based on mutual respect, trust, and a dedication to spiritual development. Even though the guru-disciple relationship is fundamental to traditional Tantra, it is essential to approach it with insight and ethical considerations.

Tantra recognizes the unity of the universe and all living things. The interconnectivity principle emphasizes the notion that one's actions can have a Individuals have an impact on the consciousness of the group. Tantric practitioners participate in activities that foster empathy, compassion, and service because they understand that they must benefit the world. The Tantric view of the interwoven web of life is consistent with the practice of qualities like kindness, generosity, and non-harming.

In summary, Tantra is a deep spiritual philosophy that goes beyond its common connotations of sexuality and exotic activities. Fundamentally, Tantra recognizes the holiness inherent in every moment and the interaction of energy and consciousness with the divine in all facets of life. Tantra's core teachings include. The balancing of masculine and feminine energies.The development of mindfulness. The activation of Kundalini energy. The practice of holy sexuality. The recognition of the interdependence of all living things. Tantra invites people to connect with life fully and set out on a path of personal and relational development by providing a holistic approach to spirituality that integrates human existence's mental, bodily, and spiritual aspects.

Mindfulness techniques for enhancing sexual experiences

The intersection of mindfulness and sexuality has garnered an increasing amount of interest in the area of human experience. This is because individuals seek ways to strengthen their connection with themselves and their partners. Mindfulness, which originates in ancient practices of contemplation, entails developing a heightened awareness of the current moment without passing judgment on it. The application of this concept to sexuality paves the way for a more profound comprehension of one's wants, sensations, and emotional responses. This essay examines various mindfulness strategies that can be utilized to improve sexual encounters. Particular attention is paid to the significance of present, communication, and self- awareness.

Being present is one of the fundamental concepts of mindfulness, and it is a robust technique that may be utilized in the context of sexual experiences. Intimate moments allow individuals to fully immerse themselves in the sensory parts of the experience when they are totally present during those moments. To do this, it is necessary to redirect the attention away from distractions, worries, or preconceived notions. This will allow for the cultivation of a profound connection with the physical and emotional aspects of the current experience. Engaging the senses will enable individuals to increase the intensity of their experiences, heighten the pleasure they experience, and establish a more personal connection with their bodies as well as the bodies of their partners.

The practice of mindful breathing, which is an essential component of mindfulness practices, is a critical component for the enhancement of sexual encounters. Not only can deep and focused breathing help to relax the nervous system, but it also helps to heighten awareness of the feelings that occur within the body. Within this approach, participants are encouraged to synchronize their breath with the rhythm of their movements, producing a harmonic and connected experience. Releasing stress, being attuned to their partner's cues, and maintaining a continuous flow of energy throughout the encounter are all possible outcomes that can be achieved by persons who concentrate on their inhale and exhalation.

The practice of mindfulness also emphasizes the significance of non-judgmental awareness, which has the potential to be transformative when applied to sexual experiences. It is common for people to have expectations, fears, or judgments regarding their bodies, aspirations, or performance associated with these aspects of themselves. Through mindfulness, one is encouraged to let go of these judgments and embrace both oneself and one's partner for compassion. Having this acceptance creates a secure environment for being vulnerable and honest, which in turn helps to cultivate a more profound emotional connection and makes it possible to conduct a more in-depth investigation of one's wants and boundaries.

Effective communication is of the utmost importance in any relationship, but it takes on an even greater level of significance when it comes to sexual sexual experiences. Expressing one's desires, boundaries, and sentiments in a clear and empathic way is an essential component of mindful communication. When individuals are aware of both verbal and non-verbal signs, they can establish an atmosphere that promotes open communication, increasing the level of mutual understanding and trust between them. The practice of mindful communication during intimate times not only guarantees consent but also enhances the overall experience by bringing the intents and desires of partners into alignment.

Techniques of mindfulness can also be utilized to address obstacles such as anxiety related to performance or difficulties in maintaining arousal. Individuals can interrupt the cycle of worry and self- doubt by shifting their attention away from worrisome thoughts and concentrating on the moment they are experiencing. The practice of mindfulness is beneficial in that it enables one to accept the ebb and flow of sexual encounters and to recognize that these experiences can differ from one encounter to the next. This non- judgmental approach to sexual experiences has the potential to reduce the amount of pressure placed on performance and to create an environment that is more relaxed and enjoyable.

In addition, the practice of incorporating mindfulness into sexual interactions has the potential to strengthen the link between the mind and the body. A significant number of people, frequently as a result of stress or previous traumatic experiences, deal with dissociation or separation during intimate moments. Individuals can help themselves reconnect with their bodies through mindfulness, creating a sense of embodiment and presence. Body scan meditations are one example of such a practice. Through the process of reintegrating physical sensations with emotional and mental awareness, this reintegration makes it possible to have an experience that is more holistic and satisfying.

Furthermore, mindfulness promotes a curious and exploratory frame of mind, which helps cultivate a sense of originality and inventiveness in sexual experiences. Individuals can break free from routine and preconceived conceptions when they approach each interaction with a beginner's mindset. This paves the way for a more spontaneous and adventurous discovery of pleasure. Individuals are encouraged to let go of their expectations and accept the unknown when they adopt this mindset, which creates an environment conducive to the growth of discovery and connection.

In conclusion, the incorporation of mindfulness practices into sexual experiences provides. A comprehensive approach to the development of more profound relationships. The enhancement of pleasure.The resolution of any difficulties that may emerge.

Through the cultivation of the present, the incorporation of mindful breathing, the acceptance of non-judgmental awareness, the practice of effective communication, and the reconnection with the body, individuals can build a sexual life that is more intimate and meaningful. When it comes to sexuality, mindfulness is not about accomplishing a particular objective; instead, it is about appreciating the journey, accepting vulnerability, and cultivating a genuine connection with oneself and one's partner. The potential for personal development, self-discovery, and enhanced relationships is becoming increasingly apparent as individuals continue to investigate the subtle dance between sexuality and mindfulness.

Cultivating presence and awareness in intimate moments

Cultivating presence and awareness in intimate times is extremely important, especially in our fast-paced world when distractions are common and daily expectations can be daunting. A transforming journey towards a deeper connection with oneself and one's spouse can be found at the confluence of mindfulness and intimacy. The essential of developing presence and awareness in private moments is examined in this essay, along with its potential effects on relationships, wellbeing, and the general caliber of our most intimate encounters.

Fundamentally, intimacy necessitates a presence that transcends the material world. It entails living entirely in the now, appreciating the experience's rich sensory array, and allowing oneself to be vulnerable. Being physically present is only one aspect of cultivating presence in intimate times; another is making a mental and emotional space where distractions disappear and a deep connection with one's and partner's feelings is possible.

Cultivating presence can be effectively achieved through mindfulness, which is rooted in ancient contemplative traditions—being mindful means being aware of the current moment without judgment. When used in private, it helps people release worries, anxieties, and obsessions from the outside world and makes it easier to connect more fully with the feelings, energy, and sensations that occur at the moment. This increased awareness can give the experience a new depth and let people enjoy each moment without being distracted by regrets from the past or anxieties about the future.

Slowing down is one of the cornerstones of developing a presence in private situations. Slowing down in a society that frequently exalts efficiency and speed may seem paradoxical. But the speed of contemporary life can seep into our moments, creating a rush and a sense of impatience. People can appreciate the intricacies of shared vulnerability, the nuances of touch, and the subtleties of emotions when they take their time. This slowing down intentionally makes room for a deeper bond and closeness beyond the physical act.

An essential component of mindfulness exercises, breath serves as a link between the conscious and physical domains. People can center themselves in the present and create a rhythm synchronizing with the developing experience by focusing on their breath during intimate times. By creating a familiar rhythm between lovers, conscious breathing strengthens the bond with one's body and enhances the sense of oneness and connection. By approaching breath mindfully, one can use it to elevate awareness and presence beyond a primary function.

Investigating the senses is another aspect of cultivating the presence in private moments. Mindfulness allows people to completely appreciate all of their senses, including touch from a partner, skin smell, and the soft sounds of breathing together. People can weave a multisensory tapestry that enhances the intimate interaction by focusing on these sensory aspects. In addition to deepening the experience, this sensory awareness stabilizes people from getting lost in their thoughts and keeps them grounded in the here and now.

To cultivate presence and awareness in intimate moments, mindful contact becomes essential. It entails investigating the subtleties of pressure, warmth, and texture and developing a keen sense of touch. The goal of conscious touch is exploration driven by response and curiosity rather than following a preconceived plan. This method encourages a mutual flow of feelings and energy, enabling a dance of connection that transcends the actual physical act.

Intimate moments require self-care and couples' dynamic interaction to cultivate the present. A shared commitment to being in the moment and sensitive to one another's experiences is necessary for mindful connection. It calls for attentive listening with all of one's senses, not just the hearing. People can create a space where wants are expressed, vulnerabilities are revealed, and emotional closeness flourishes by being fully present with their partner. This shared presence lays the basis for a more meaningful connection and understanding between people.

Emotional acceptance and acknowledgment are vital components of developing consciousness during personal situations. By encouraging people to approach their emotions without judgment, mindfulness fosters an environment where people can express their feelings honestly and freely. Thanks to this emotional awareness, people can interact on profound emotional and spiritual levels in addition to physical ones. By accepting the entire range of feelings, from happiness to vulnerability, people can successfully negotiate the complexities of private times by being genuine and transparent.

There are difficulties involved in developing a presence during private exchanges. Keeping your attention in the here and now may be challenging because the mind is easily distracted and can wander. People who practice mindfulness are encouraged to face these distractions gently and without judgment of themselves. By regular practice, people can teach their thoughts to return to the present moment, cultivating a higher consciousness that is more approachable during personal interactions.

In summary, developing awareness and presence during personal moments is a life-changing experience beyond closeness's sensual qualities. It entails consciously embracing vulnerability, being present, and cultivating a close relationship with oneself and one's spouse. Throughout this journey, mindfulness provides practices that help people stay rooted in the abundance of the present. People who explore this possibility open themselves to a deeper, more genuine, and satisfying intimacy experience that improves their relationships and general wellbeing.

CHAPTER VI

Transcending Pleasure and Pain

Examining the dual nature of pleasure and pain

Pleasure and pain are two opposing elements in the complex tapestry of the human experience, dancing together to create our emotions, perceptions, and, ultimately, how we view life. This essay explores the complex relationship between pleasure and suffering, their psychological foundations, and the valuable insights they can provide into the human condition.

Despite being viewed as opposites, pleasure and pain

are strangely interwoven into the fabric of our lives. An essential feature of human nature is the pursuit of pleasure, which motivates people to look for happiness, contentment, and fulfillment. Whether from intellectual pursuits, emotional ties, or sensory delights, pleasure becomes a compass that directs our decisions, interpersonal interactions, and general well-being. However, in this quest, suffering is an unavoidable sidekick—an essential component of the human experience that gives our life richness, contrast, and purpose.

The biological basis of pleasure and pain is their sensory

component. The release of neurotransmitters like dopamine, which produces emotions of reward and encourages actions that result in positive results, is frequently linked to pleasure. Contrarily, pain triggers the body's stress response and compels action to avoid or lessen the source of discomfort since it perceives it as a threat or injury. This dual system is an evolutionary adaptation that keeps us safe by directing us away from possible threats and toward experiences that will be useful to us.

Pleasure and pain have a profound psychological complexity that extends beyond the biological domain. These experiences are highly personal due to their subjective nature, shaped by societal conventions, cultural influences, and unique viewpoints. In all its manifestations, pleasure is an individualized reaction to stimuli; what makes one person happy might not make another feel the same way. Similarly, each person experiences pain differently, as it is a complex emotional and physical sensation. Recognizing the variety of human experiences and the complex interactions between psychological variables that influence our perceptions is necessary to comprehend the subjective nature of pleasure and misery.

The way that pleasure promotes social ties and connections is one feature of pleasure that goes beyond the individual. In communities, shared joys foster a sense of cohesion and connection, whether they take the shape of joint celebrations, artistic endeavors, or life events. Pleasure becomes a means of interaction, relationship-building, and connection, adding to human cultures' social fabric. But because pleasure is a communal experience, it can also have positive and negative effects. Individual pursuits of pleasure can be shaped by societal norms and expectations, which can either promote or impede personal fulfillment.

On the other hand, pain—which is sometimes thought of as a solitary experience—can create strong bonds between people. Common difficulties forge relationships that surpass individual differences, sympathetic reactions to suffering, and group initiatives to lessen misery. In all its manifestations, pain is a unifying force that reminds us of our shared vulnerability and the interdependence of all human experience. Understanding that others are in pain encourages empathy, compassion, and a shared duty to relieve suffering, highlighting the possibility of group development and unity.

Throughout history, the dual nature of pleasure and sorrow has been deeply intertwined in literature, art, and other creative expressions. Artists, writers, and other creators frequently exploit the tension between joy and suffering to explore the intricacies of the human brain, provoke strong emotional reactions, and question social norms. Through its ability to reflect the subtleties of pleasure and pain, art becomes a mirror that invites people to face, consider, and make sense of the disparate yet interconnected parts of their lives.

Examining the emotional terrain of happiness and suffering shows how they dynamically relate to resilience and personal development. As a source of contentment and delight, pleasure enhances good emotions, promoting resilience and overall well-being. But being pain-free does not mean that life is without difficulties or problems. Adversity and pain, in actuality, frequently act as stimulants for resilience, personal development, and the creation of coping strategies. Emotional maturity, self-awareness, and the ability to deal with life's unavoidable complications are all influenced by one's ability to negotiate difficult situations and draw lessons from them.

Philosophical discourse has always addressed the dichotomy of pleasure and pain, posing queries like the essence of contentment, the yearning for a significant life, and the significance of pain in the human condition. For example, practical philosophies assert that maximizing pleasure and minimizing misery is the ultimate purpose of human conduct. But this practical viewpoint ignores the depth to which suffering contributes to our comprehension of the world and ourselves, oversimplifying the complexity of the human experience.

Conversely, existentialist philosophers explore the existential significance of facing life's inevitable difficulties, such as grief and sorrow. According to the existentialist perspective, finding meaning in life requires negotiating the complexity of this dual nature, which is intrinsically marked by pleasure and misery. Existentialism emphasizes the possibility of human agency and the creation of meaning amid hardship while encouraging people to face the existential reality of their lives. It acknowledges the inevitable nature of pain.

The complex dynamics of love, desire, and intimacy in interpersonal relationships are manifestations of the dual nature of pleasure and sorrow. The complexity of love relationships, where happiness, passion, and fulfillment combine with the possibility of heartbreak, disappointment, and emotional agony, frequently entangles the quest for pleasure. People vulnerable enough to open themselves to love run the risk of experiencing happiness and sadness, which emphasizes the broad spectrum of emotions that define close relationships.

The ability to communicate effectively, have emotional intelligence, and be open to vulnerability are all necessary for navigating the intricacies of pleasure and pain in relationships. Over time, the depth and resiliency of connections are shaped by the shared experiences of joy and sadness, which constitute an essential part of the fabric of relationships. When a couple navigates the dual nature of pleasure and suffering with empathy and understanding for one another, they frequently discover that the difficulties deepen their relationship and promote a journey of intimacy and progress.

In summary, the analysis of the complementary character of pleasure and suffering points to a deep interdependency that shapes the human experience. These complex interactions, which are rooted in philosophy, psychology, culture, and biology, influence how we perceive the world and relate to others. Even though they are sometimes seen as opposites, pleasure and suffering work together in a sophisticated dance that gives our lives more depth, significance, and richness; accepting that pleasure and agony have two sides helps people deal with life's challenges with resiliency, self-awareness, and a deep appreciation for the beauty resulting from conflicting forces

Transforming challenges into opportunities for growth.

By its very nature, life is packed with difficulties, roadblocks, and unknowns that put people's fortitude to the test. However, these difficulties also present a significant chance for personal development and transformation. This essay examines the skill of turning setbacks into learning experiences by exploring the mental processes, coping methods, and philosophical viewpoints that enable people to overcome hardship and come out stronger, smarter, and more resilient on the other side.

Adversity can elicit a spectrum of feelings, ranging from frustration and despair to worry and terror, depending on whether it manifests as personal setbacks, professional problems, or unanticipated life occurrences. Challenges can transform people, depending on how they respond to and view them. A change in perspective that sees difficulties as chances for development rather than as insurmountable barriers might open the door to a life-changing experience.

Psychologically, turning obstacles into learning opportunities frequently requires resilience, or an individual's capacity to overcome adversity, overcome failures, and carry on in the face of difficulty. Instead of being a natural quality, resilience is a talent that can be developed and reinforced via self-awareness, coping mechanisms, and an optimistic mindset. When people embrace obstacles as inevitable parts of life, they may approach them with a perspective that sees opportunities for growth, development, and personal evolution.

Furthermore, turning obstacles into opportunities requires cognitive reframing. This entails purposefully changing how one views hardship and redefining it as an opportunity to learn new things, gain wisdom, or better understand oneself. People can find significance in problems and see them as stepping stones rather than roadblocks on the way to growth by changing the narrative from victimization to empowerment.

In the workplace, obstacles frequently take the form of abrupt setbacks, job changes, or the requirement to pick up new skills in a setting that is changing quickly. Taking on these difficulties as chances for professional growth can result in improved abilities, flexibility, and a comprehensive range of capabilities. People who see obstacles as opportunities to grow frequently find that they can better deal with the dynamic and ever-changing nature of the workplace.

Relationships within the family are not exempt from difficulties. Distress can arise from interpersonal disagreements, communication breakdowns, or unavoidable relationship changes. However, relationships can be profoundly deepened when obstacles are seen as chances for more empathy, understanding, and connection. Adversity often acts as a stimulus for a couple's bond to expand and become a more resilient partnership when they embrace problems as cooperative opportunities for growth.

Global crises, political upheaval, and economic downturns are examples of societal problems that offer group development and transformation opportunities. As communities band together to tackle issues cooperatively, a shared sense of accountability and a dedication to creating a more resilient and inclusive society are fostered, and societal resilience is born. Communities can grow the collective resilience to not only endure storms but also emerge more muscular, more unified, and better prepared to face future difficulties when they face the crucible of adversity.

Philosophical viewpoints from several traditions and schools of thought provide significant insights for converting obstacles into chances for development. For example, stoicism advises people to recognize that problems are inevitable and to use them as opportunities to develop characteristics like courage, wisdom, and resilience. The Stoic school of thought strongly emphasizes that although people may not be able to influence external circumstances, they do have power over how they see and react to those circumstances.

Similarly, existentialist ideologies emphasize how accepting obstacles as necessary parts of the human experience can have a transformational effect. Existentialists contend that people can define their identities, find purpose in life, and forge their pathways by facing the inherent uncertainties, hardships, and existential difficulties that confront them. From an existential standpoint, challenges are like canvases on which people paint the stories of their lives, giving them meaning and purpose.

The growth mindset, which psychologist Carol Dweck coined, emphasizes how critical it is to view obstacles as chances for growth and learning. Those with a growth mindset enthusiastically welcome challenges because they view them as opportunities to develop new skills rather than limitations. This way of thinking encourages a love of learning, fortitude in the face of adversity, and the conviction that hard work and persistence may result in ongoing progress.

Spiritual viewpoints can also provide insightful information about how to turn obstacles into chances for personal development. Adversity is often seen as a tool for spiritual growth and purification in many spiritual traditions. People can find comfort, strength, and direction in spiritual ideas through prayer, meditation, or contemplative practices. These beliefs build a feeling of transcendence and purpose that helps people face obstacles with more excellent composure.

Overcoming obstacles leads to transformation, a dynamic interaction of psychological, emotional, and philosophical elements rather than a sequential process. With their roots in age-old contemplative traditions, mindfulness practices help people develop present-moment awareness and the ability to accept difficulties without passing judgment. People may negotiate the complexity of adversity with better resilience and clarity if they face challenges with an open heart and a focused intellect.

The process of transforming oneself through adversity frequently entails reflection and self-discovery. Adversity causes people to reevaluate their objectives, values, and life decisions. Self-reflection can help people understand their strengths, limitations, and fundamental values better. This understanding can then help them realign their lives with authenticity and a sense of purpose.

Social support is essential to convert obstacles into chances for development. Mutual understanding and a sense of community are fostered through engaging in support networks, seeking mentorship from experienced individuals, and connecting with others who have had the same difficulties. People can take strength from one another and work together to traverse the challenges of their journeys in a collaborative environment fostered by sharing experiences, insights, and coping mechanisms.

In summary, turning obstacles into learning opportunities is a dynamic and multifaceted process that calls for psychological fortitude, a reframing of the situation from a cognitive perspective, and a philosophical perspective that views adversity as a necessary component of the human experience. Seeing obstacles as opportunities for personal, professional, or societal advancement enables people to face life's uncertainties with fortitude, flexibility, and a dedication to lifelong learning. In the end, people can develop the inner strength, resilience, and wisdom necessary to set out on a transforming path toward both personal and collective growth through the furnace of adversity.

Navigating the complexities of desire and attachment

Desire and attachment are vital threads in the tapestry of human interactions and emotions, influencing our worldview. This essay examines the intricate relationship between desire and attachment, its psychological roots, and its significant effects on human life.

Desire, typically seen as the motivation for pleasure, connection, and fulfillment, drives people toward objectives, relationships, and experiences. Desire, rooted in biology and psychology, ranges from transitory impulses of immediate satisfaction to life-changing longings. It is physical, emotional, and intellectual and is essential to human contact.

Desire is complex because it changes. Acute requirements or stimuli trigger transient desires, while persistent desires are life goals. Desire is often driven by anticipation, excitement, and the hope of wholeness. Desire might conflict with societal norms, ethical issues, or personal ideals, creating a difficult balance between gratification and restraint.

However, attachment is the emotional tie between people that typically brings stability, warmth, and belonging. Our evolutionary history shows that attachment between caregivers and newborns improves survival. Attachment patterns affect interactions with friends, romantic partners, and social groups as people age, altering how they connect, relate, and form emotional attachments.

Desire drives people to interact and experience, but attachment provides security and emotional connection. Attachment affects how people see the world, their emotional well-being, and their relationships. Early attachment patterns can shape adult relationships.

The relationship between desire and attachment is complex and ambiguous. Desire can motivate people to try new things, but attachment can make them reluctant to let go, causing tensions between personal goals and solid relationships. Managing desire and attachment is a delicate dance that defines relationships, self-discovery, and personal fulfillment.

Exploring the psychological roots of desire and attachment shows how they affect cognition and emotion. Cognitive psychology links desire to how people see and understand the world. Cognitive processes, including attention, memory, and decision-making, shape wants and determine what people like or dislike.

Attachment, however, is crucial to emotional regulation and self-confidence. Attachment theory, developed by John Bowlby and Mary Ainsworth, holds that early caregiver experiences establish internal working models—mental representations of self and others that determine relationship expectations. Secure attachment builds trust, but insecure attachment might cause interpersonal discomfort, avoidance, or ambivalence. Psychological theories like Maslow's hierarchy of needs illuminate human motivations in desire. Maslow postulated a pyramid of human needs, starting with physiological demands and ending with higher-order needs like self-actualization and transcendence. This concept states that unfulfilled needs drive the desire for fulfillment and self-expression.

Psychodynamic theories, including Freudian id, ego, and superego, help explain desire. According to Freud, the id wants rapid fulfillment based on unconscious urges and impulses. The ego mediates the id's desires and social rules. The superego's internalized morality adds conscience to decision-making.

These viewpoints are supported by attachment theory,

which emphasizes emotional attachments in relationships as essential to human growth. Early caregiver interactions shape attachment patterns and later relationship dynamic control. These tendencies affect how people express and respond to desires in intimate relationships.

As people navigate desire and attachment, awareness

becomes useful. Without judgment, mindfulness allows people to notice their thoughts, feelings and wants without reacting. This heightened awareness will enable people to reflect on their desires and attachment patterns, helping them understand their motivations and how they affect relationships.

Mindfulness allows people to examine their needs

without becoming obsessed with them, noting cravings' transience and the self's change. Non-judgmental knowledge of attachment patterns will enable people to analyze how past experiences may affect their current relationships and desires. Meditation and contemplative exercises help people balance desire and attachment.

Ancient knowledge of modern existential thought on

desire and attachment philosophy is rich. The Bhagavad Gita, a critical Hindu book, discusses desire as a motivator and source of suffering. It argues that desire can lead to self-realization and spiritual growth when treated with duty and egolessness.

Buddhist teachings, especially the Four Noble Truths,

examine desire and attachment as causes of suffering. Buddhism teaches that understanding desire, craving, and attachment and cultivating non-attachment to end the cycle of suffering leads to enlightenment.

Existentialist philosophers like Jean-Paul Sartre and Albert Camus examine the conflict between freedom and human limitations. Existentialists encourage people to face life's uncertainties, make accurate decisions, and own their impulses and relationships. It stresses self- awareness and intentional living in the face of desire and attachment's existential concerns.

In contemporary psychology, "secure base," drawn from attachment theory, adds a relational component to desire and attachment. A solid base, usually provided by a caregiver in early life, allows exploration and desire pursuit. This applies to adulthood, where stable ties offer emotional support and motivation to achieve goals and overcome obstacles.

Cultural and societal forces complicate desire and attachment. Cultural norms influence how people express desires and form attachment bonds, determining what is acceptable or taboo in relationships. Social expectations, gender roles, and familial factors complicate wants and attachments, changing individuals' identities and relationships.

The conflict between personal liberty and emotional connection significantly complicates romantic relationships. Early romantic involvement is generally marked by intense desire, motivated by infatuation and new relationships. As partnerships develop, attachment dynamics become more critical, affecting emotional investment, commitment, and resilience.

Desires and attachment patterns might conflict, raising problems about autonomy, independence, and identity in a partnership. Effective communication, mutual understanding, and a willingness to negotiate changing emotions and expectations are needed to balance personal desires and shared attachments.

In conclusion, desire and connection play a multifaceted role in human experience. Passion drives people toward connection, fulfillment, and self-expression. Emotional attachment provides security, belonging, and a framework for interpersonal issues. The delicate tango between these forces requires self-discovery, attention, and deliberate life.

Understanding the psychology of desire and attachment

shows how cognitive processes, emotional regulation, and prior experiences affect these forces. Mindfulness helps people cultivate awareness and balance, allowing them to approach cravings and attachments intentionally.

Philosophical viewpoints deepen and illuminate desire

and attachment. Philosophy invites people to consider desire, attachments, and intentional life as a means of progress and self-realization, from ancient literature to modern existential thought.

Norms, expectations, and human interactions form

desire and attachment narratives in culture and society. Recognition of these external effects complicates the individual journey of navigating desires and developing ties.

Desire and attachment are a canvas on which people

paint their lives. Finding balance—embracing desires with mindfulness, navigating attachments with intention, and constructing a story of personal growth, resilience, and meaningful connections—is the art.

CHAPTER VII

The Alchemy of Intimacy

Exploring the transformative power of intimate connections

Our ability to connect, especially in deep relationships, shapes our existence. These relationships change our identities, affecting personal growth, resilience, and self-discovery beyond emotional resonance. This essay examines the psychological, emotional, and existential changes that result from close relationships.

The dance of vulnerability and trust underpins intimate relationships. Intimacy lets people share their actual emotions, anxieties and wants. Vulnerability builds trust, which is essential for meaningful partnerships. Trust creates a safe area where people feel accepted, respected, and understood, enabling transformation.

Emotional reciprocity underpins intimate bonds' transforming ability. Shared experiences, mutual support, and compassionate understanding weave close relationships into a dynamic, expressive dance. One partner's emotions can affect the other's views, attitudes, and coping techniques. Personal growth can result from this emotional symbiosis as people overcome problems, celebrate successes, and evolve together.

Through personal relationships, people can learn more about themselves. A trusted partner's reflection helps one recognize strengths, limitations, and growth opportunities. Through personal relationships, people often discover parts of themselves that were hidden in other circumstances, leading to self-awareness.

Managing common issues is where deep connections truly transform. Intimate relationships allow people to share their abilities and resources when facing external or internal challenges. Mutual support and encouragement build resilience, helping partners face challenges together. Close relationships help you survive, grow, and learn to cope in times of trouble.

Intimate relationships give life significance. We want deep, meaningful ties as humans. Close connections allow people to contemplate existential concerns, life's transience, identity, and purpose. The journey with a companion adds depth and meaning to life.

Intimate interactions shape identities through reciprocal influence. People co-create each other's beliefs, values, and views as they navigate relationships. Sharing experiences, dreams, and problems creates a shared story that defines each relationship. Individuals affect their own and their spouses' transformations.

Intimate ties also change the physical world. Close relationships improve health and well-being, according to research. Positive personal relationships reduce stress, boost immunity, and extend life. Physical well-being from close connections reinforces the interconnectedness of mind and body and the idea that transformative processes occur at numerous levels of human experience.

Sharing joy and achievement and navigating conflict and vulnerability are essential to building personal relationships. When handled effectively, conflict can help a relationship grow. Conflict resolution improves communication, understanding, and partner bonding. Vulnerability and conflict can shape personal relationships into lasting partnerships.

Sexuality, a crucial part of personal relationships, enhances their transforming power. Sexual intimacy strengthens relationships and creates a connection that goes beyond the ordinary. Exploring desires, boundaries, and mutual satisfaction improves sexual and emotional closeness.

Attachment theory illuminates how emotional links shape personal relationships. Attachment theory, developed by John Bowlby and extended by Mary Ainsworth, holds that early caregiver experiences influence an individual's attachment style, affecting adult relationships. Based on trust and emotional reactivity, secure attachments encourage exploration and personal growth.

However, insecure attachments—characterized by fear, avoidance, or ambivalence—can hinder personal change in intimate relationships. Insecure attachment styles can cause trust, rejection, and vulnerability issues. Therefore, strong attachments that support individual and relational growth are essential to the transformational power of intimate connections.

Philosophies on intimate relationships offer everlasting insight across nations and eras. The ancient Greek word "philia," meaning close friendship or attachment, emphasizes the transformational power of personal relationships. In his Nicomachean Ethics, Aristotle praises philia as fundamental to human flourishing, highlighting the reciprocal impact of deep ties on well-being and moral progress.

Jean-Paul Sartre and Simone de Beauvoir explore authenticity, freedom, and the intertwining of individual destinies to explore the transformational power of close connections. Existentialists believe intimate relationships are essential to finding meaning and purpose in life. Spiritual traditions recognize the transformational potential of profound love bonds.

Integrating spiritual growth into everyday relationships

Relationships are potent catalysts for self-discovery and progress. When infused with spiritual awareness, these relationships become transcendent, inviting people to examine their souls and transform. This essay examines how integrating spiritual growth into daily relationships can deepen, enrich, and resonate relationships.

Recognizing a shared core that transcends individual identities is vital to partnership spiritual growth. Spiritual awareness helps people see the connectedness of all beings and the common thread that unites us. This recognition promotes empathy, compassion, and profound connection in relationships. Relationships become spiritual inquiry and mutual progress when people recognize this common core.

Spiritual growth in relationships requires presence, attentiveness, and conscious awareness. These attributes enable people to engage with their spouses, friends, and family truly. Presence is awareness of the other person's emotional, mental, and spiritual qualities. High awareness helps spiritual progress by deepening connections and creating a shared consciousness.

Contemplative traditions teach mindfulness, which is essential to spiritual growth in relationships. Being present in the now without judgment or attachment to the past or future is mindfulness. Mindfulness in relationships needs active listening, non-reactive communication, and appreciation of the richness of each moment with a loved one. Mindfulness in relationships gives the ordinary sacredness.

Communication, a foundation of any relationship, becomes sacred when informed by spirituality. Communicating effectively for spiritual growth requires profound listening, empathy, and expression. Hearing and understanding another's experiences builds emotional closeness and a deeper connection.

Communication promotes spiritual growth by fostering understanding, compassion, and meaning-making.

Unconditional love—transcending circumstances, shortcomings, and imperfections—is essential to relationship spiritual growth. Spiritual understanding of the interconnectedness of all existence and the divine energy within each being underpins unconditional love. When people build unconditional love in relationships, they make space for acceptance, forgiveness, and a transforming love that transcends ego and embraces the spiritual core of self and others.

Integrating spiritual growth into relationships transforms how they handle obstacles and conflicts. Every relationship has issues, but the spiritual approach encourages people to see them as growing opportunities. From a spiritual standpoint, disputes represent self-repair needs. The mindful handling of relationship issues becomes a sacred self-discovery and mutual progress process.

Many spiritual traditions emphasize forgiveness, which is essential to relational spiritual progress. Release animosity, give up retaliation, and embrace compassion to forgive. Forgiveness in relationships heals, renews, and restores harmony. Forgiving oneself and others elevates the relationship spiritually, allowing it to move forward gracefully.

Spiritual growth strengthens romantic relationships and makes them precious. Sacred or spiritual partnerships emphasize that relationships can awaken and enlighten both parties. Spiritually growing partnerships encourage each other's travels, nurture consciousness, and embrace the union's transforming power.

Parenting offers a unique opportunity for spiritual growth. Spiritually oriented-parenting instills empathy, compassion, and mindfulness in children. Encourage children to explore their spiritual identities, develop connection, and model conscious living to help parents and children grow spiritually. Family ties are laboratories for moral development and life's mysteries.

Spiritual growth also helps friendships, the hidden heroes of personal support systems. Conscious, spiritually educated friendships celebrate each other's uniqueness, embrace mutual growth, and explore more profound levels of existence. Friendships that support one other's spiritual journeys are sources of inspiration, insight, and mystical experiences.

The diversity of spiritual practices and traditions enhances the transformational power of spiritual growth in everyday relationships. Meditation, prayer, rituals, and contemplative exercises help people develop spirituality and deepen relationships. These spiritual rituals encourage us to be present, show thanks, and be compassionate, enriching our relationships.

Buddhism and Hinduism illuminate interconnection and the value of relationships in spiritual growth. Dharma—cosmic order or duty—emphasizes the web of relationships and ethical obligations that people have to one another. Recognizing and appreciating dharma in relationships transforms spiritual growth.

Love is essential to spiritual progress in relationships, according to Christianity. The biblical mandate to "love thy neighbor as thyself" and the emphasis on agape love demonstrate the transformational power of unconditional love. These teachings apply to relationships via practicing love as a spiritual practice, transcending ego, and embracing the divine in oneself and others.

Existentialist philosophy emphasizes personal responsibility and meaning-making, which offers a unique viewpoint on spiritual progress in relationships. Existentialists like Jean-Paul Sartre and Albert Camus believe people may create their fates and give their lives significance. Existentialists choose to co-create meaning, purpose, and spiritual growth in relationships.

Mindfulness, based on Buddhist philosophy and popularized in modern times, helps partnerships grow spiritually. Mindfulness requires awareness, nonjudgment, and acceptance. Mindfulness practices like conscious breathing, listening, and deliberate presence offer a sacred place for connection and spiritual growth in relationships.

Finally, spiritual growth raises everyday relationships with the divine. With awareness, presence, and a commitment to mutual progress, partnerships may alter individuals and societies. The profound journey of discovering humanity's interconnectedness fosters empathy, compassion, and spiritual fulfillment. As people intentionally spiritualize their connections, They uncover their selves, grow together, and realize the spiritual potential in every connection.

Alchemical practices for deepening connection

Alchemy, the ancient art and philosophy of turning base metals into gold, is full of symbolic insight. Alchemy is related to self-transformation and spiritual development beyond its literal goals. As this essay investigates, alchemical practices can be metaphors for strengthening self- and social connection. Alchemical symbols like transmutation, purification, and the union of opposites can transform relationships and inspire spiritual progress.

Alchemical methods for enhancing connection focus on transmutation—transforming one's base traits into higher, more refined ones. Transmutation in relationships entails examining and improving traits that may limit connection. This procedure is alchemically similar to distillation, which purifies the essential by separating impurities. Self-reflection helps people recognize and release personality traits that define honest relationship connections. Distillation allows for deeper, more genuine relationships and self-transformation.

Alchemy also emphasizes purification, which removes impurities and refines one's essence. Relationship purification releases unpleasant emotions, previous grievances, and limiting ideas that prevent connection. This alchemical process demands purposeful emotional and spiritual cleansing, allowing people to approach partnerships with a clean heart and mind. Deep and sincere relationships can be fostered by eliminating emotional baggage and purifying the soul.

Alchemy's alchemical wedding, the marriage of opposites, strengthens relationships. This philosophy recognizes human duality and integrates competing forces for harmony and balance. The union of opposites in relationships accepts one's and one's partner's good and dark sides. Embracing human complexity helps you understand and appreciate each person's unique qualities, fostering a more harmonious relationship.

Synergy in relationships resembles the alchemical process of conjunction, which unites antagonistic forces. Synergy argues that working together can yield more than the sum of individual contributions. Alchemical synergy occurs when varied characteristics, skills, and viewpoints are combined in a relationship. People contribute to the alchemical process of conjunction by recognizing and valuing each partner's talents and differences, producing a dynamic and transformational connection.

Alchemists think the philosopher's stone can turn base metals into gold and provide immortality. The philosopher's stone symbolizes inner harmony, wisdom, and self-realization, the culmination of the alchemical path. In relationships, partners encourage each other's self-discovery and spiritual progress while they search for the philosopher's stone. Pursuing the philosopher's stone in relationships requires mutual transformation, lifting the connection to a higher degree of understanding and purpose.

The alchemical symbol of the ouroboros—a serpent eating its tail—represents cyclical regeneration and life's endless cycle. In relationships, the ouroboros symbolize growth and change. Alchemical activities like the ouroboros repeat self-reflection, purification, and union to strengthen the connection. As people and partners change, they contribute to the relationship's alchemical process, keeping it alive and adaptable to human experience.

The alchemical element mercury, associated with metamorphosis and fluidity, is used flexibly in relationships. Relationships must adapt to change like mercury. Alchemical practices promote relationship mobility and recognize that change is inevitable. Adaptability helps people handle interpersonal changes gracefully, leading to alchemical progress and growth.

The alchemical concept of nigredo, or blackening, represents the beginning of decomposition and breakdown to make a place for the new. In relationships, nigredo means confronting and deconstructing toxic behaviors, old-fashioned ideas, and emotional blocks that prevent intimacy. Alchemical disintegration requires facing one's and the relationship's darkness to renew and regenerate. Nigredo is essential to connection alchemical metamorphosis.

Alchemical processes of albedo (whitening) and rubedo (reddening) purify and refine the changed substance. Albedo symbolizes connection, knowledge, clarity, and cleansing. Communication, empathy, and connection improve with practice. Alchemical whitening creates the way for rubedo, where love, passion, and spiritual illumination infuse the bond. At the end of the alchemical journey, relationships glow red, symbolizing the richness and depth of shared experiences.

Relationships can be deepened using alchemy as a metaphor. Modern psychology, especially depth psychology, uses alchemical symbolism to explore how human connections change. Jung, a pioneer in depth psychology, used alchemical principles to explain individuation—the process of self-realization and integration of the unconscious. Individualization and alchemical methods for increasing connection emphasize self-awareness, mutual growth, and the integration of competing psyche energies in partnerships.

Using alchemical techniques to increase connection

takes intentional intention, self-reflection, and reciprocal engagement. Alchemical connection journeyers embrace development and regeneration through ongoing transformation. Alchemical lenses encourage people to see relationships as living, breathing beings capable of tremendous growth and spiritual alchemy.

In conclusion, alchemical processes provide a rich model

for relationship strengthening. Transmutation, purification, and opposites lead to self-discovery and other discoveries in the alchemical path. Alchemy can guide people on a sacred quest for connection, contributing to the endless cycle of growth, regeneration, and spiritual evolution in human connections.

CHAPTER VIII

Sacred Sensuality and Personal Empowerment

Embracing personal empowerment through sacred sensuality

Sensuality and empowerment weave a rich tapestry of self-discovery and growth in human experience. Sacred sensuality invites people to explore their sensual selves in alignment with their higher purpose. This essay explores the transformative journey of embracing personal empowerment through sacred sensuality and how this intimate connection can help people understand themselves, form authentic relationships, and improve their well-being.

Conscious synthesis of physical, emotional, and spiritual sensual sensations is sacred sensuality. It redefines sexuality and encourages people to cherish their hot selves. This view transforms sensuality into a tool for self-love, empowerment, and discovering one's desires and boundaries.

Accepting one's body and passions is critical to holy sensuality and personal empowerment. Social expectations, cultural taboos, and excessive beauty standards can make people alienated from their bodies and judge or humiliate sensuality. Reclaiming body agency, releasing cultural conditioning, and nurturing a good relationship with the sensual self are the first steps to personal empowerment.

Personal empowerment via sacred sensuality requires self-discovery beyond social limits. It entails exploring desires, preferences, and boundaries by oneself. This exploration includes emotional and spiritual sensuality as well as bodily feelings. People empower themselves through self-awareness and honesty by exploring what offers joy, contentment, and connection.

Mindfulness helps strengthen oneself through spiritual sensuality. Mindfulness lets people experience their senses by establishing a non-judgmental awareness of the present. Mindfulness deepens the sensory connection with the body, emotions, and wants. Being present in the sensual experience can deepen self-awareness and empower the mind, body, and spirit.

Personal empowerment through sacred sensuality recognizes the link between sensuality and self-love. Explore your sensual self with curiosity and acceptance to build a healthy self-image. This journey embraces the body as a sacred vessel for pleasure, joy, and connection. Self-love prepares people for empowerment from a deep wellspring of self-acceptance and admiration.

Cultural and cultural myths sometimes pit sexuality against spirituality. The integration of sacred sensuality accepts that these realms can coexist. Spirituality is an individual's connection to a greater purpose, a transcendent knowledge of existence, or a sense of interconnection with the cosmos. Embracing holy sensuality empowers the individual by recognizing the spiritual dimension in sensual encounters and nourishing both the physical and spiritual self.

Sacred sensuality often overlaps with spiritual traditions that honor the human body and sensual experiences. Tantric traditions emphasize the blending of male and feminine energies as a road to spiritual enlightenment through sexuality. Tantric concepts can help people discover themselves, balance energy, and feel empowered.

In mythologies and spiritual traditions, sexuality is typically symbolized as a potent force for change and empowerment. Many civilizations celebrate the holy feminine, which respects femininity's divinity and sensuality's creative energy. To empower yourself through divine sensuality, align with these archetypal energies, and use their knowledge for self-discovery and progress.

Integrating holy sensuality into intimate relationships fosters authenticity. Sensuality empowers people to be self-aware and sincere in their interactions. Healthy, mutually rewarding relationships need openly communicating desires and boundaries without shame or judgment. Personal empowerment through sacred sensuality helps create partnerships that honor each partner's sensual self.

Deep emotional attachments and intimate interactions are also part of sacred sensuality. In consenting, respectful interactions, people can practice intimacy and connection. Mindful contact, intentional communication, and shared wants foster trust and vulnerability. Personal empowerment via holy sensuality in intimate relationships creates physically, emotionally, and spiritually gratifying relationships.

In personal healing, holy sensuality transforms. With reverence and attention, sensuality can release emotional barriers, trauma, and negative conditioning. Sensual self-care, such as aware breathing, self-massage, or holy rituals, helps reconnect with the body and promote emotional well-being. Personal empowerment via divine sensuality leads to physical, emotional, and spiritual healing.

Remember that achieving personal empowerment through sacred sensuality is a unique path. No one technique empowers and delights everyone. Curiosity, self-compassion, and nonjudgment of one's sensual journey are crucial. Allowing oneself to explore and embrace the hot self can lead to real and self-loving empowerment.

Finally, sacred sensuality empowers the bodily, emotional, and spiritual self. Reclaiming body autonomy, increasing mindfulness, and experiencing sensuality in line with actual wants are the goals of this method. This holy journey helps people create a more robust and liberated sense of self that embraces sensuality as a path to self-discovery, authentic connections with others, and well-being.

Overcoming societal conditioning around sexuality

Social conventions, cultural expectations, and historical perspectives shape sexuality, a fundamental human trait. Society strongly influences sexual attitudes, beliefs, and practices. Society has long imposed strong sex standards, stigmas, and taboos, producing a complicated landscape that affects individual expression, relationships, and well-being. This essay discusses cultural sexuality conditioning and how individuals can overcome it to have more open, honest, and unrestrained sexuality.

Sexuality is conditioned early in life by education, religion, and culture. Sexual expression norms are learned from childhood. Early imprints shape sexual identities and how people view their bodies, wants, and relationships. Gender norms and prejudices often influence how people should display their sexuality, establishing a binary framework that may constrain various and fluid identities.

Religion has long shaped sexual attitudes. Sex is often linked to morality and fertility in many religions. This effect can make people with non-traditional sexual encounters feel guilty, ashamed, or inadequate. To overcome sexuality conditioning, one must balance religious beliefs and personal autonomy, acknowledging the diversity of opinions and the value of individual agency in intimacy.

Cultural taboos further complicate societal conditioning by shaping what is acceptable and unacceptable. Conversations about sex are sometimes uncomfortable or silent, limiting free dialogue and enlightenment. Lack of discourse encourages falsehoods, ignorance, and sexuality stigma. Overcoming cultural conditioning requires addressing these taboos, promoting open talks, and building inclusive, sex-positive places for understanding and acceptance.

Media's ubiquitous effect reinforces social standards and shapes sexuality beliefs. Mainstream media promotes unrealistic beauty, intimacy, and relationship standards, causing unease and inadequacy. Skewed or sensationalized portrayals of sexual orientations, identities, and practices marginalize those who don't fit society. Media literacy, critical thinking, and diverse and inclusive sexuality representations are needed to overcome societal conditioning.

Sexual orientation is strongly conditioned by society, with heteronormativity generally assumed. LGBTQ+ people may struggle to overcome societal conditioning that marginalizes or pathologizes non-heteronormative sexuality. To achieve acceptance, recognition, and equal rights, we must oppose discrimination, promote inclusivity, and celebrate sexual orientation variety.

Sexuality education and awareness must change to overcome social conditioning. Comprehensive and inclusive sex education is essential for dispelling stereotypes and myths and promoting healthy sexuality. Sexual education should encompass biological characteristics, consent, communication, diversity, and embracing one's unique sexual identity. By providing factual information, society can help break down societal conditioning.

Body positivity challenges restrictive beauty standards and social conditioning. This movement promotes body positivity in all ways. The body positivity movement changes sexuality views by advocating a more inclusive definition of beauty. Accepting varied body representations creates a more inclusive and accepting atmosphere, eliminating detrimental conditioning that may cause body shame or sexual insecurity.

Feminism has championed women's autonomy and agency to challenge sexuality conditioning. Feminists emphasize consent, deconstructing patriarchal systems that perpetuate harmful standards and sexual liberty. Feminism promotes sexual equality and empowerment by questioning power imbalances, promoting reproductive rights, and addressing sexual assault.

Sex-positivity—the view that consensual and diverse sexual expressions are natural and healthy—helps overcome social conditioning. Sex-positivity promotes open discussions about desires, preferences, and boundaries, allowing people to explore their sexuality without shame. A sex-positive worldview challenges social taboos, dismantles stigmas, and promotes the belief that sexual pleasure and well-being are vital to an entire existence.

Personal narratives and storytelling help overcome sexual indoctrination. Diversity and authenticity weave a complex tapestry of experiences that challenge preconceptions and inspire empathy. Sharing their self-discovery, acceptance, and liberation journeys helps others find sexual empowerment by creating a culture that values personal narratives.

Mindfulness helps people transcend social conditioning by increasing self-awareness and presence. Mindfulness allows people to grasp society's norms by observing their thoughts, feelings, and reactions without judgment. Mindfulness in sexuality can help people disentangle conditioning, question assumptions, and connect more authentically with their desires and boundaries.

The intersectionality of societal conditioning demands acknowledging how race, ethnicity, class, and ability affect sexuality. An inclusive strategy that respects community concerns is needed to overcome societal conditioning. Intersectional viewpoints magnify multiple voices, helping us grasp how social norms affect people of different social identities.

Psychotherapy and counseling help people overcome sexual conditioning. People can discuss their beliefs, anxieties, and desires in a secure and nonjudgmental environment with mental health specialists. Through therapy, people can acquire understanding, develop coping techniques, and feel more empowered and liberated in sexuality.

Online networks and platforms for sexual education and empowerment have made sexuality discussions more accessible. These locations offer knowledge, resources, and supportive groups that question social conditioning and offer inclusive sexuality viewpoints. Online forums promote activism, advocacy, and various sexual expressions.

In conclusion, changing sexuality conditioning takes a diverse approach and individual and social dedication. Society may liberate and empower sexuality by confronting stereotypes, supporting inclusivity, sex education, and different narratives. Self-awareness, mindfulness, support, and open communication can help individuals break free from societal restraints and have more accurate and liberated sexuality. Dismantling negative conditioning and promoting sexual empowerment creates a more inclusive and affirming society that recognizes sexual diversity.

Aligning personal desires with spiritual goals

The quest for spiritual satisfaction and the pursuit of personal pleasures frequently appear as separate paths in the complex dance of human existence. But synthesizing these seemingly disparate elements is a meaningful path with the possibility of leading a happy and meaningful life. This essay delves into the transformational potential of discovering unity between life's material and spiritual components, examining the complex process of lining up human desires with spiritual goals.

A sophisticated comprehension of both domains is the first step towards coordinating one's aspirations with spiritual objectives. Individual preferences, cultural influences, and life experiences all contribute to the many needs, wants, and aspirations that makeup one's wishes. These goals might be anything from monetary ambitions to emotional contentment, professional achievement, or the search for deep connections. Conversely, spiritual objectives encompass the quest for personal development, establishing a link with the divine, and realizing one's greater self. The interaction of these two dimensions creates the setting for a life-changing experience that encourages people to investigate the fusion of their spiritual and material selves.

Realizing these elements are not intrinsically conflicting is fundamental to balancing spiritual aspirations with personal needs. Social narratives frequently maintain a dualism between achieving financial success and developing spiritually, portraying both as opposing goals. But when people accept that life's material and spiritual facets may coexist and benefit one another, the dualism vanishes. The problematic part is actively navigating this integration to make sure that one's desires line up with spiritual teachings and create a prosperous and meaningful existence.

A key component of many spiritual traditions,

mindfulness is a beacon of guidance on the alignment path. Cultivating present-moment awareness, objective observation, and inner self-awareness are all components of mindfulness. People who practice mindfulness become more aware of their motivations, wants, and the faint hints of their spiritual yearnings. This self-awareness becomes a compass that helps people identify the desires that align with their true selves and advance their spiritual development.

The Eastern philosophical idea of Dharma provides

essential insights into balancing material aspirations with spiritual objectives. Dharma, which is frequently translated as cosmic order or duty, strongly emphasizes living in accordance with one's actual nature and achieving one's particular role in the vast scheme of things. Understanding how one's aspirations contribute to the greater whole, acknowledging and honoring one's Dharma, and making sure that efforts are in line with the core values of one's spiritual path are all necessary for bringing one's wants into alignment with spiritual goals.

A purposeful analysis of one's values leads to the

alignment process. Values are guiding concepts that represent what matters most to a particular person. People can assess their goals and behaviors by clarifying and prioritizing their values. A sense of integrity and purpose in all endeavors is fostered by intentionally reflecting on whether one's objectives correspond with sincerely held values, which is necessary to align personal desires with spiritual aspirations.

When approached with awareness and ethical

considerations, material success—frequently a component of human desires—does not conflict with spiritual growth. One can consider the amassing of money, professional accomplishments, or material belongings as a means to an end rather than an aim in and of itself. Pursuing personal desires becomes a vehicle for spiritual expression when people infuse their practical endeavors with a spiritual intention, such as promoting compassion, improving the well-being of others, or supporting worthwhile causes.

Finding fulfilling relationships is a basic human need with much room for spiritual development. Relationships can be used as testing grounds for expressing compassion, self-discovery, and spiritual principles. Establishing connections that foster growth on both sides, authenticity, and joint pursuit of greater truths is essential to bringing one's wants for love, friendship, and connection into harmony with spiritual aspirations. Relationships are significant in helping people's desires and spiritual aspirations align when they become a source of inspiration and spiritual companionship.

Many spiritual traditions support the practice of gratitude, which can be a transformational tool in bringing one's wants and aspirations into alignment. Gratitude cultivation entails recognizing and appreciating the wealth in one's life. Gratitude helps people change their perspective from what they lack to what they have, which leads to contentment and a stronger spiritual bond. Gratitude practice offers a prism through which individual goals can be seen in light of the previously bestowed favors, promoting a sense of fulfillment beyond monetary gains.

Alignment becomes fundamental to simplicity, a concept promoted in spiritual teachings from many cultural perspectives. Decluttering the material and mental worlds, making room for spiritual activities, introspection, and a closer relationship with one's desires are all aspects of simplifying one's life. The deliberate pursuit of simplicity encourages people to distinguish between necessary and unnecessary wants, concentrating on what is most in line with their spiritual path.

How obstacles and failures are handled demonstrates the transformational effect of aligning personal aspirations with spiritual objectives. Because life is dynamic, people can encounter difficulties, experience setbacks, or have unmet expectations. From a spiritual standpoint, obstacles present chances for development and self-awareness. When a person's spiritual aspirations and personal wants are in harmony, it creates a strong base that enables them to rise above hardship, grow from failures, and see roadblocks as opportunities for personal growth.

Integrating one's spiritual aspirations with personal desires is a continuous process that calls for constant introspection and improvement. Naturally, as people grow in their spiritual awareness, so too may their desires. The alignment path is fluid and dynamic partly because of regular self-evaluation, meditative practices, and a dedication to ongoing learning. Accepting that growth is cyclical enables people to modify their aspirations to align with their developing spiritual understanding.

To sum up, integrating one's spiritual aspirations with personal aspirations is a life-changing process encouraging people to integrate their spiritual and material selves. On this journey, guiding principles include mindfulness, value clarification, the pursuit of meaningful connections, gratitude, simplicity, and resilience in the face of adversity. People construct a monetarily affluent and spiritually purposeful life when they intentionally manage the interaction between their aspirations and spiritual ambitions. The alignment process leads to a harmonic integration of the human experience by fostering a sense of fulfillment, authenticity, and interconnectedness.

CHAPTER IX

Challenges and Solutions in the Journey

Common challenges on the path of sacred sensuality

Sacred sensuality is a transforming path of profound self-discovery and connection as it weaves together human existence's physical, emotional, and spiritual aspects. Nevertheless, the journey towards sacred sensuality has challenges, just like any significant investigation. Cultural taboos around sensuality, personal insecurity, and societal conditioning frequently cause these obstacles. This essay explores the many obstacles people encounter while pursuing sacred sensuality, including how interpersonal dynamics, self- perception, and social pressures can obstruct a more genuine, in-depth relationship with one's sensual self.

The influence of social conditioning on personal perceptions of sensuality and sexuality is a common obstacle on the road to sacred sensuality. Narrow and restrictive ideas about what is considered acceptable or forbidden in terms of sensuality can be perpetuated by society, which is frequently affected by cultural, religious, and historical traditions. Messages of guilt, shame, or objectification of the body can seep into the brain and erect obstacles that prevent a person from expressing their sensuality freely. It takes deliberate work to question and relearn these deeply rooted beliefs to break free from societal conditioning and make room for a more accurate and accessible relationship with sexuality.

The persistent conflict in specific cultural and theological frameworks between the spiritual and the sensual presents another prevalent challenge. Some religious systems distinguish between human life's spiritual and material facets, which causes people to view sensuality as fundamentally distinct from the divine. When people explore their sensual side, this paradox can lead to internal tensions and feelings of guilt or shame. Taking a holistic approach that acknowledges sensuality as a sacred and essential part of the human experience that is inextricably linked to spiritual development is necessary to overcome this obstacle.

The obstacles that arise on the path of sacred sensuality are primarily influenced by one's opinion of oneself and body. Insecurities thrive when cultural norms and societal standards lead to skewed ideas about what makes one attractive and desirable. Negative self-talk, body shame, or judgmental fear can all be obstacles that prevent people from freely and joyfully expressing their sensuality. To overcome this obstacle, one must practice body positivity, self-love, and a mentality that values each person's individuality and natural beauty regardless of what others think.

Communication and consent can be problematic in the context of sacred sensuality, especially in interpersonal relationships. A healthy and consensual exploration of sexuality requires open and honest communication about expectations, boundaries, and wants. However, social conventions that stigmatize candid discussions about sex and sensuality can obstruct productive debate. The authenticity and safety of the sensual experience may be jeopardized when people conceal their wants or negotiate intimate times without clear communication out of fear of rejection or criticism. To overcome this obstacle, there has to be a societal shift that de-stigmatizes discussions about sensuality and promotes open communication and consent in romantic partnerships.

Another obstacle to sacred pleasure is navigating the intricacies of interpersonal dynamics. Disparities in expectations, comfort zones, or wants between partners can lead to conflict and prevent a peaceful exploration of sensuality. Furthermore, cultural conventions frequently impose strict responsibilities and expectations on partners in partnerships, which may stifle each partner's uniqueness and authenticity in expressing their sensuality. Fostering an atmosphere of respect for one another, candid communication, and a shared dedication to the study of sensuality as a cooperative and enjoyable journey for both partners are necessary to overcome this obstacle.

The effects of prior traumas or unfavorable experiences might present severe obstacles to sacred sensuality. People may be carrying emotional scars from relationships in the past, from societal conditioning, or from events in which they felt violated or ashamed. Emotional obstacles resulting from these experiences may impede one's capacity to trust, show vulnerability, or fully explore sensuality. It takes a therapeutic and caring approach to address this issue, focusing on self-awareness, healing, and the progressive reclaiming of one's sensual agency in a secure setting.

Sensual taboos in culture and religion add to the difficulties experienced by individuals pursuing spiritual investigation. Social norms that specify acceptable and unacceptable levels of sensuality might engender emotions such as guilt, humiliation, or fear of being judged. Those who are afraid of being shunned or called abnormal may find it difficult to express and embrace their sensual sides. To overcome this obstacle, we must question and demolish these taboos through activism, education, and the development of a more tolerant and inclusive cultural narrative about pleasure.

The modern world's hectic schedule and high expectations can hinder virtuous sensuality. Stress from the workplace, hectic schedules, and the continual barrage of stimuli can cause people to lose touch with or disregard their sensual selves. Sacred sensuality is cultivated via deliberate moments of present, awareness, and self-care—all of which can be difficult to prioritize in a society that frequently puts material success before one's needs. It will need deliberate effort to set aside time for introspection, rest, and the development of pleasurable experiences that feed the body, mind, and soul to overcome this obstacle.

The mainstream media's commercialization and objectification of sensuality can lead to inflated expectations and obstacles in sacrosanct inquiry. A limited and idealized vision of sensuality is frequently presented in media representations, reinforcing stereotypes and elevating irrational ideals of desire and beauty. People can experience pressure to live up to these ideals, which could cause them to feel inadequate or cut off from their true sensual selves. To overcome this obstacle, one must develop media literacy, question distorted images, and embrace a broader, more varied definition of sensuality that values individuality and inclusivity.

One major obstacle that prevents people from pursuing sacred sensuality is the absence of inclusive and thorough sex education. People who are not adequately educated about sensuality, pleasure, and consent may find it challenging to manage their boundaries and wants. A lack of a comprehensive awareness of sensuality can lead to ignorance, guilt, and insecurity about pursuing one's sensual identity. A cultural shift toward sex-positive, all-encompassing education that provides people with the correct knowledge encourages candid communication. It cultivates a healthy concept of sensuality, which is necessary to overcome this obstacle.

In summary, obstacles might arise in sacred sensuality due to various factors, including cultural taboos, self-perception, interpersonal dynamics, past traumas, and societal conditioning. To overcome these obstacles, a deliberate and purposeful commitment to self-love, healing, open communication, and developing a more tolerant and inclusive cultural narrative surrounding sensuality are necessary. Accepting the difficulties encountered on the road of sacred sensuality facilitates a better awareness of oneself. This allows for a liberated and genuine study of sensuality based on mindfulness, respect, and a celebration of the many forms human sensuality can take.

Practical solutions and guidance for overcoming obstacles

Life, with its rich tapestry of events, offers a variety of difficulties and trials that can put our bravery, adaptability, and resilience to the test. Obstacles are a natural part of the human journey, whether emotional difficulties, professional difficulties, or personal disappointments. This essay delves into valuable strategies and advice for conquering life's challenges. It offers insights into developing a resilient attitude, promoting emotional health, and navigating personal development challenges.

Developing a resilient mindset is one of the keystones for conquering life's challenges. The capacity to overcome hardship, adjust, and get more robust in the face of difficulties is resilience. They are adopting a mindset that views challenges as chances for learning and development rather than insurmountable impediments, essential to building resilience. Reframing obstacles as transient and overcomeable and seeing that failures are necessary for a more excellent journey toward personal development are the first steps in this mindset shift. Through developing resilience, people can use hardship as a tool to advance themselves, viewing obstacles as opportunities rather than roadblocks.

The discipline of mindfulness, which has its roots in old-fashioned contemplative traditions, provides valuable strategies for overcoming challenges in life with awareness and grace. Being mindful entails paying attention to one's thoughts and feelings while stepping back from judgment. People can improve their clarity, emotional control, and self-awareness by integrating mindfulness into their daily lives. The practice of mindfulness enables one to respond to challenges in a calm and collected manner. People can approach obstacles with a calm and concentrated mind, permitting more effective problem-solving and decision-making instead of becoming mired in the story of struggle.

Overcoming life's challenges requires emotional wellbeing, and mental and emotional resilience requires self-compassion. Being self-compassionate is being nice and understanding to oneself, particularly when facing obstacles. By embracing their challenges with warmth and acceptance, people can practice self-compassion instead of thinking negative or condemning thoughts about themselves. By fostering a supportive internal environment, this practice helps people become more emotionally resilient by giving them the confidence to take on issues head-on and believe they can overcome them.

Strategic planning and goal-setting offer helpful advice for overcoming problems in life with direction and purpose. By dividing more complex issues into smaller, more achievable objectives, people can chart a course for advancement. By establishing attainable goals, people can progress gradually and feel a sense of achievement that increases their motivation. Strategic planning also entails foreseeing probable roadblocks and creating backup measures. This proactive approach promotes control and readiness in the face of uncertainty by giving people the means to overcome obstacles.

Creating a network of support is essential to conquering challenges in life. Human relationships offer a variety of viewpoints that illuminate possible answers, as well as emotional support and encouragement. Opening up to mentors, family members, or trusted friends enables people to discuss their struggles, gain insightful knowledge, and get the help they need to overcome obstacles. A support system is vital not just because of the joys that are shared among members but also because of the resilience that develops when members face life's challenges together.

Learning from failures becomes a fundamental component of human development as one strives to overcome difficulties. Every obstacle provides insightful teachings that support flexibility, resilience, and self-discovery. People can find trends, strengths, and opportunities for development by reflecting on their past experiences, both successful and unsuccessful. Through introspection, people become more self-aware and acquire the knowledge necessary to overcome challenges in the future. Adopting a mindset of perpetual learning converts challenges into chances for growth and progress.

Developing an upbeat and hopeful mindset is a valuable strategy for conquering challenges in life. Rather than denying the existence of difficulties, positive thinking modifies how those difficulties are seen. People can go from thinking like victims to thinking like empowered persons by concentrating on possibilities, growth, and solutions. Positive energy is a motivating factor that propels people to overcome challenges and confront problems head-on. This upbeat viewpoint affects people's wellbeing and helps foster a more positive and productive atmosphere conducive to conquering common obstacles.

The resilience of the mind and emotions is closely associated with physical wellbeing. Developing a healthy lifestyle that includes regular exercise, a balanced diet, and enough sleep lays a strong foundation for overcoming problems in life. Energy levels, concentration, and emotional control are all influenced by physical wellbeing. Participating in physical activity that enhances one's health fortifies the body and mind, giving one the energy and endurance required to meet obstacles head-on.

Gratitude practice provides a transforming viewpoint

that can strengthen resilience when faced with life's challenges. Despite difficulties, gratitude is acknowledging and valuing life's good things. Practicing gratitude helps people change their perspective from what they lack to what they have, which promotes abundance and resilience. Having gratitude helps people overcome challenges by reminding them of their abilities, assets, and support networks. It also helps people realize how interwoven life's events are and how to appreciate each moment for what it is.

Being adaptable is essential for conquering challenges in

life in a world that is changing quickly. Success in both the personal and professional spheres depends on having the flexibility to adapt to changing conditions, welcome uncertainty, and overcome unforeseen obstacles. A resilient, flexible, and open-minded mindset is essential to developing adaptability. One must also be willing to learn from adversity. People who accept change as a given in life can face challenges with curiosity and adaptation, seeing them as chances for personal development and evolution.

Seeking expert advice or mentorship gives people

access to outside viewpoints, knowledge, and insightful advice on overcoming particular obstacles. Experts, mentors, or coaches can provide direction based on their experiences, offering a road map for skillfully overcoming challenges. Formulating strategic plans and better comprehending problems and possible solutions can benefit from the unbiased advice of a reliable advisor. Getting assistance from people with the necessary experience can help you overcome challenges with more competence and self-assurance.

In all its forms, spirituality can be a powerful source of

support and direction for overcoming challenges in life. Many people find that their spiritual beliefs provide a framework for deciphering obstacles' greater meaning and purpose. Prayer, meditation, and mindfulness are examples of spiritual practices that can offer comfort, grit, and a sense of being a part of something more than oneself. A strong sense of inner serenity, purpose, and an understanding of the interconnectedness of all life experiences can be fostered by incorporating spiritual elements into conquering challenges.

To sum up, conquering life's challenges is a complex process that calls for an all-encompassing strategy that includes mental toughness, emotional stability, thoughtful preparation, dependable connections, ongoing education, physical wellbeing, optimism, thankfulness, flexibility, expert advice, and spiritual mooring. Through adopting pragmatic solutions and assistance in these domains, individuals can more effortlessly manage challenges, developing a mindset that converts impediments into chances for personal development, adaptability, and a deeper comprehension of the complex dance of life.

Building resilience in the face of setbacks

Life is a complex journey of problems and accomplishments with unanticipated turns. Setbacks are a necessary part of life; they put our grit, tenacity, and ability to evolve to the test. Developing resilience in the face of failures shows to be a critical ability that enables people to face hardships head-on, grow from them, and come out stronger on the other side. The many facets of resilience are examined in this essay, covering the psychological, emotional, and practical elements that play a role in developing this vital trait.

Resilience is fundamentally the capacity to overcome hardship and constructively adjust in the face of setbacks. It entails the dynamic interaction of behavioral, emotional, and cognitive elements that influence how a person reacts to difficulties. Keeping an optimistic outlook is one of resilience's most critical psychological components. Developing optimism and self-belief in one's capacity to overcome challenges can be a strong anchor in trying circumstances. This optimistic perspective improves emotional health and modifies how failures are perceived, viewing them as chances for development rather than insurmountable obstacles.

Successfully navigating and managing emotions is closely related to emotional resilience. A wide range of emotions, including disappointment, annoyance, melancholy, and even rage, are frequently triggered by setbacks. Acknowledging, comprehending, and practicing self-regulation of these emotions are all necessary for building emotional resilience. This dynamic control helps people stay balanced throughout difficult situations and keeps emotional storms from impairing their general health. Accepting emotions as a regular aspect of life helps people develop a resilient mentality that promotes flexibility and inner strength.

The development of self-awareness facilitates the process of constructing resilience. Understanding oneself—including coping strategies, skills, and weaknesses—lays the groundwork for overcoming obstacles. When faced with obstacles, self-aware people can identify their cognitive patterns, emotional reactions, and behavioral habits. This realization serves as a self-management tool, empowering people to make deliberate decisions that support their values and long-term objectives even in the face of hardship.

Developing realistic coping mechanisms is essential to enhancing resilience. These tactics include asking for help from others, using good communication techniques, and problem-solving abilities. People who can recognize practical solutions, express their demands, and seek assistance when faced with obstacles are more likely to overcome the barriers and succeed in life. The use of resilience in practice is taking an active approach to challenges, being dedicated to finding solutions, and seeing that failures are not insurmountable roadblocks but rather chances for innovative solutions.

It becomes clear that social support is an essential

external component in building resilience. Human connection offers a safety net in trying times, whether it takes the shape of friends, family, or a larger group. An individual's resilience can be significantly enhanced by the shared experiences, emotional support, and encouragement from being part of a supportive network. In addition, asking for assistance or connecting with those going through a similar situation helps people feel like they belong and are not alone in their troubles.

The ability to change with the times is known as

adaptability, a crucial component in resilience building. Because life is unpredictable, people frequently need to reevaluate their objectives or approaches in response to setbacks. Individuals who can adjust to changing circumstances, modify strategies, and adopt a flexible mindset are more likely to withstand life's challenges. The resilience of a resilient attitude is enhanced by the capacity to let go of inflexible expectations and accept life's ups and downs.

Resilient people are characterized by their ability to

learn from failures. Resilient people perceive failures and difficulties as chances for learning and development rather than as indicators of inadequacies. A never-ending cycle of improvement is facilitated by reflection on failures and readiness to draw conclusions and lessons from them. Every obstacle becomes a learning opportunity that offers insightful criticism for improving tactics, developing abilities, and expanding self-awareness. When failures are turned into opportunities for personal and professional growth, they cease to be mere impediments.

Taking personal responsibility is essential to developing resilience. People can take control of their stories by accepting responsibility for their choices, actions, and reactions to failures. Resilient people understand their agency in handling difficulties rather than giving in to a victim attitude. This sense of accountability also extends to the decisions made in the face of failures, encouraging an empowered and proactive strategy supporting resilience growth.

Different forms of spirituality can offer a deep context

for developing resilience. Many people find comfort, meaning, and a sense of connectedness to something more than themselves in their spiritual beliefs. Prayer, meditation, and mindfulness are examples of spiritual practices that can be sources of support when things get tough. Integrating spiritual concepts like faith, surrender, and acceptance helps people build a resilient mindset that sees beyond their current problems and connects them to a larger view of life's journey.

The process of developing resilience makes the

importance of one's values clear. Values act as tenets that direct conduct and decision-making. Resilient people ensure that their behaviors are consistent with their guiding principles so that failures do not undermine their morality or sense of direction. Living a values-driven life gives people clarity and a resilient mindset that keeps them grounded in their authenticity and purpose, even in adversity.

With its roots in contemplative traditions, mindfulness

provides valuable techniques for increasing resilience through awareness of the present moment. Mindfulness entails developing a vigilant and impartial consciousness of one's ideas, feelings, and environment. People can learn to respond to setbacks with more clarity, discernment, and emotional control by engaging in mindfulness practices. Resilient people have a resilient attitude rooted in the present moment because they can remain present in the face of hardship, preventing them from being overcome by negative thoughts or anxieties about the future.

In summary, developing resilience in the face of adversity is a multifaceted process that includes practical, psychological, and emotional components. Keeping an optimistic viewpoint, controlling emotions, growing self-awareness, and embracing useful coping mechanisms are all part of cultivating a resilient mindset. Resilience is mainly shaped by external influences, including social support, adaptability, and the capacity to learn from mistakes. The development of a resilient mindset also involves the use of mindfulness, spirituality, personal accountability, and alignment with values. By integrating these many components, people can effectively traverse setbacks and emerge from obstacles not just uninjured but also altered and strengthened by the lessons they have learned.

CHAPTER X

Embracing the Path of Enlightenment

The connection between sacred sensuality and enlightenment

Throughout history, the quest for enlightenment—a condition of profound spiritual awakening and elevated consciousness—has been a critical goal in many spiritual traditions. The integration of holy sensuality—a deep, conscious connection with one's sensual and sexual self—as a route to enlightenment is one facet that has frequently been discussed in this journey. This essay explores how sensual energy exploration and knowledge may be transformative in pursuing spiritual illumination, delving into the complex relationship between sacred sensuality and enlightenment.

The understanding that the human body, frequently viewed as merely a vessel in certain spiritual traditions, is a sacred and essential component of the spiritual path is at the core of the relationship between holy sensuality and enlightenment. Those who practice sacred sensuality are encouraged to see their bodies as means of experiencing and expressing divine energy rather than as barriers to spiritual development. People begin a journey that eliminates the artificial division between the physical and the spiritual by accepting and appreciating the intrinsic holiness of sensuality. This leads to a more comprehensive and complete view of the self.

The ancient spiritual practice of Tantra, which has its roots in Buddhist and Hindu philosophy, provides significant insights into the relationship between enlightenment and pleasure. Tantra sees the human body as a microcosm of the cosmos, complete with sensual and sexual aspects. Tantra practice is embracing and transmuting the energy inherent in sensuality to transcend dualities, such as pain and pleasure. Tantra seeks to awaken the dormant spiritual force at the base of the spine called Kundalini through rituals, breathwork, and conscious connection with the body. Kundalini energy is said to ascend via the chakras, resulting in a state of elevated consciousness and spiritual enlightenment.

Being mindful becomes a fundamental practice on the path to enlightenment when combined with divine sensuality. Cultivating mindfulness entails being more present and aware of everything at all times. When applied to sensuality, mindfulness enables people to completely experience each sense—taste, smell, sight, and sound—savoring every moment. People can connect with the divine energy that permeates all elements of creation and transcend mental limits by being fully present in sensuous moments. By bringing people into the present and enabling a direct experience of the holy in the sensual, mindfulness in sacred sensuality opens doors to enlightenment.

The study of sacred sensuality also touches on the idea of divine union, which is fundamental in many mystic traditions. A transcendent aim in the quest for enlightenment is uniting with the cosmic energy or the religious. Sacred sensuality invites people to acknowledge the divine presence in both themselves and their partners, offering a concrete and experiential route to this union. People can feel a profound sense of unity, transcending the bounds of ego and experiencing the interconnectedness of all life through conscious and intentional connection with sensory energy. Holy sensuality thus takes on the form of a sacred dance of connection, reflecting the cosmic dance of creation and destruction.

Taoism, an old Chinese philosophy, also provides insightful information about the relationship between sensuality and enlightenment. The idea of Yin and Yang is used in Taoist teachings to represent the dynamic interaction of opposites, such as the feminine and masculine energy. It is believed that reaching balance and enlightenment requires individuals to cultivate and harmonize these energies within themselves. In Taoism, sacred sensuality entails the development of sexual energy, or Jing, via exercises like Qi Gong and Taoist sexual methods. It is thought that the transformation of sexual energy nourishes the body, harmonizes Yin and Yang, and results in spiritual enlightenment. To achieve vitality, longevity, and spiritual illumination, Taoist sages stressed the significance of engaging with sexuality in a deliberate and aware manner.

The teachings of many mystics and spiritual authorities also make clear the relationship between enlightenment and divine sensuality. The route to enlightenment in Sufism, the mystical school of Islam, revolves around Divine Love. Sufi poets and mystics frequently compared the soul's longing for oneness with the Divine to sensual, romantic love to illustrate how powerful and transformational this longing is. In the framework of Divine Love, the study of sensuality takes on a symbolic and experiential quality as people strive to transcend their egos and unite with the infinite via the language of their hearts.

The Bhakti spiritual tradition in India acknowledges the transformational power of sensuality on the path to enlightenment while emphasizing devotion and love for the Divine. Bhakti poets and practitioners frequently use sensual and expressive language to convey their passion for the Divine. It is believed that having a profoundly physical and emotional relationship with the Divine is a legitimate and effective way to achieve spiritual enlightenment. To achieve a state of ecstasy and dissolution of the ego, followers of the Bhakti tradition engage in intense devotion and the visceral sensation of love.

Sacred sensuality explored within the Enlightenment framework is not exclusive to Eastern spiritual traditions. The idea of unity with the Divine also exists in Western mystical traditions, such as Kabbalah, the mystical branch of Judaism. A symbolic depiction of the universe, the Kabbalistic Tree of Life has passageways linking the heavenly and terrestrial domains. Sensuality research is a way to take physical encounters to a higher plane of consciousness. Within the Kabbalistic tradition, people aim to reach a higher consciousness and climb the spiritual ladder by intentionally interacting with life's sensory parts.

The fusion of enlightenment and sacred sensuality is also evident in contemporary spiritual practices prioritizing embodied spirituality. According to teachers and practitioners in modern spiritual traditions, sensuality can be a doorway to higher consciousness and spiritual illumination. Conscious sexuality, tantra classes, and thoughtful sensual interaction are being accepted more and more as means of bringing about individual and societal change. By recognizing the connection between the mental, emotional, and spiritual facets of the human experience, these contemporary methods promote a more inclusive and holistic route to enlightenment.

It is understood that the relationship between sacred sensuality and enlightenment is about engaging with life's sensuous elements in a conscious, purposeful, and attentive manner rather than indulgence or hedonism. It entails realizing that the body is a temple through which the divine can be experienced and that sexuality is a sacred expression of life force energy. Enlightenment ideals are aligned with the deliberate study of pleasure to transcend the ego's limitations, dissolve dualities, and understand the interconnectedness of all things.

In conclusion, a universal thread woven through diverse spiritual traditions and practices demonstrates the fundamental relationship between sacred sensuality and enlightenment. Sensuality exploration becomes a powerful and transformational route to enlightenment, whether derived from the ancient knowledge of Tantra, the philosophical insights of Taoism, the mystical expressions of Sufism and Bhakti, or the modern embrace of embodied spirituality. People can experience the divine inside themselves and the world around them by consciously acknowledging sensuality's inherent holiness and engaging with it. This journey removes the illusion of separation. Sacred sensuality invites people to dance with the holy in every facet of their sensual and spiritual journey. It is a doorway to enlightenment and a lively, rich tapestry of human experience.

Integrating spiritual insights into daily life

Spiritual growth invites people to discover their inner selves and connect with a more significant, transcendent reality beyond religious borders. Spirituality is not just introspection or sacred rituals but the seamless integration of spiritual truths into our daily lives. As this article shows, integrating spiritual insights into everyday life can improve well-being, establish authentic connections, and give ordinary times a profound sense of purpose.

Integrating spiritual insights into daily life requires a paradigm shift—an awareness that the commonplace and the holy are not incompatible. Spirituality encourages people to see the divine daily and find meaning and purpose. This transformation begins with mindfulness, developed through meditation, contemplation, or attentive breathing. By being present in each moment, people allow spiritual insights to enter their consciousness, turning mundane tasks into chances for connection, growth, and profound self-discovery.

Gratitude is a crucial method to incorporate spirituality into daily living. Gratitude is a strong spiritual discipline that appreciates the riches in each moment. By intentionally cultivating thankfulness for life's people, events, and challenges, people focus on what they have rather than what they lack. Graciousness makes everyday life seem spectacular, creating contentment and connectedness with life's richness. Gratitude makes simple things like eating, spending time with loved ones, and admiring nature sacred.

When used daily, spiritual truths like compassion and empathy help create a more compassionate and linked society. Empathy and understanding are possible when people recognize the shared human experience, including its pleasures and tragedies. Spiritual insights frequently emphasize the interconnectedness of all life, encouraging compassion for oneself and others. Kindness, tiny or enormous, becomes a visible representation of spiritual understanding, creating a ripple effect that raises consciousness and makes society more compassionate.

Spiritually-based mindful living entails genuine engagement with each moment. This involves acting on personal beliefs and spiritual principles to live with integrity and sincerity. Mindful living encourages people to consider how their activities affect themselves and others. Spiritual insights into decision-making help people transcend ego-driven cravings and live more intentionally.

Spiritual insights can be integrated into daily life through mindfulness in conversation. Mindful communication requires attentive listening and intentional speech. Being present in conversations deepens relationships and fosters respect. Spiritual insights in communication go beyond words; they acknowledge the divine inside each person, allowing for authentic expression and active listening. Daily, mindful communication promotes harmony, conflict resolution, and meaningful connections.

Inner serenity and resilience are linked to spiritual integration into daily life. Spiritual activities stress a calm mind detached from external events. Spiritually integrated people draw on inner stillness and resilience when faced with obstacles. Meditation, prayer, and other contemplative practices bring comfort and guidance, helping people handle life's challenges gracefully.

Conscious consumerism is another way to incorporate spirituality into daily life. It requires purposeful and intentional consumption of material commodities, information, media, and thoughts. Mindful consumption makes people consider how their decisions affect the environment, health, and society. Consuming spiritual principles like simplicity, gratitude, and sustainability helps people live more mindfully and harmoniously across the globe.

Lifelong learning integrates spirituality with daily living. Spiritual wisdom stresses ongoing self-discovery and growth. Spiritual seekers see every experience, good or bad, as an opportunity to grow. This approach fosters curiosity, openness, and development. Continuous learning makes the ordinary extraordinary by turning each moment into a personal and spiritual growth opportunity.

Nature is a great teacher for integrating spirituality into daily life. Spiritual traditions worldwide recognize nature's divinity. People connect with the earth's rhythm, life's cycles, and the interrelated fabric of existence through nature. Nature mirrors life's beauty, impermanence, and regeneration. A walk in the woods, a sunset, or a moving stream can brighten one's spiritual journey and enhance one's connection to the sacred.

Mindfulness makes regular rituals like eating, bathing, and commuting sacred. Mindful rituals provide everyday moments of spiritual meaning by focusing on each activity. Eating can be a thoughtful practice of gratitude for earthly food. Purification and self-care can be achieved through bathing. Commuting can be a time for quiet thought. By spiritualizing daily activities, people make the ordinary special and create a feeling of holiness in their lives.

Spiritual discoveries must be integrated into daily life through authenticity, attention, and conscious living. Aligning one's activities with one's deep wellspring of insight is more important than following rigid practices or external expectations. People intentionally use spiritual insights to create purpose, connection, and meaning in their daily lives. Life becomes a sacred adventure of self-discovery, progress, and a constant dance with the divine as the ordinary becomes a spiritual canvas.

Sustaining and deepening the journey towards enlightenment

Ancient and profound, the quest for enlightenment transcends cultural, spiritual, and philosophical borders. It invites people to explore their awareness, discover life's mysteries, and awaken spiritually. Enlightenment is a constant process that demands continued work, growing understanding, and a dedication to growth. This essay explores the timeless teachings from many spiritual traditions and contemporary viewpoints on sustaining and deepening the path to enlightenment.

Recognizing that enlightenment is a transforming process sustains and deepens the experience. To reach and retain enlightenment, awareness, comprehension, and connection with the higher self or universal consciousness must evolve. The voyage entails constant evolution, refining perception, and studying the infinite inner self. Embracing the journey's flux helps people face challenges, plateaus, and revelations with curiosity and resilience.

Mindfulness is essential to enlightenment. Contemplative traditions teach mindfulness, which increases awareness of the present. Focusing on the present lets people notice their thoughts, feelings, and sensations without judgment. A clean, non-reactive mind helps sustain the path to nirvana through mindfulness. It helps people understand the mind, eliminate ego habits, and stay in the present, where enlightenment unfolds.

The sustainable path to enlightenment centers on meditation. Buddhism, Hinduism, and contemplative Christianity use meditation to increase self-awareness and connect with the transcendent. Regular meditation helps people experience heightened consciousness, understand themselves, and find inner serenity. On the path to enlightenment, persistent meditation dissolves illusions and connects with the eternal self.

Self-inquiry and contemplation deepen the enlightenment journey by focusing inward. Self-inquiry entails investigating one's existence, thoughts, emotions, and consciousness's fundamentals. Contemplation, frequently with holy texts or intellectual musings, inspires deep reflection on universal truths. Self-reflection helps people peel down conditioning, reveal ego illusions, and discover the eternal truth that leads to enlightenment.

Sustainable and increasing enlightenment demands ethical living. Ethical principles in numerous spiritual traditions guide behaviors toward higher consciousness. Moral life promotes compassion, kindness, honesty, and integrity. Practicing these virtues creates a peaceful interior environment that fosters spiritual growth. The path to enlightenment begins with ethical behavior, which promotes inner purity and alignment with global laws.

Mindfulness in daily life sustains and deepens the path to enlightenment. People infuse spirituality into every area of their lives, not just meditation. Being present while doing daily duties, connecting with others, and facing daily problems is critical. Mindful living turns everyday activities into spiritual progress by bringing awareness into every aspect of life, sustaining and deepening the path to enlightenment.

Surrender is contradictory but powerful in the long path to enlightenment. Surrender is an active release of the ego's craving for control. Release attachments, expectations, and the illusion of separateness. Allowing life to flow and trusting the universe's knowledge helps people find their purpose. Surrendering the ego will enable people to experience divine grace that guides and deepens the path to enlightenment.

A spiritual community or sangha helps sustain and deepen the path to enlightenment. Sharing spiritual practices, meditation, and insights in a caring community helps individuals grow spiritually. A spiritual community's vitality inspires perseverance and fosters insight. The collaborative journey to enlightenment provides friendship, encouragement, and a shared resolve to awakening.

The realization that all life is interrelated supports and deepens the path to enlightenment. This consciousness, found in many spiritual traditions, transcends individuality and unites us with the universe. The corresponding vision encourages compassion for all living things, including humans and the Earth. As people realize that their awakening is interconnected to the well-being of the whole web of life, they feel inspired and motivated to reach enlightenment.

Impermanence and non-attachment sustain and deepen the path to enlightenment. Recognizing that ideas, emotions, and material goods are temporary helps people let go. Non-attachment means independence from clutching and thorough acceptance of the fleeting character of the material world. Embracing impermanence and non-attachment allows for higher spiritual insights and enlightenment.

The steady path to enlightenment is taught by nature. Reflecting on natural cycles, seasonal rhythms, and the interconnection of all living things illuminates the universal rules of existence. Nature provides a shelter for meditation, reflection, and spiritual communion by inviting people to experience the present moment. Nature helps people connect with the sacred and reach enlightenment.

Modern psychology and neuroscience support spiritual wisdom. Neuroplasticity shows the brain's ability to adapt to experiences and practices. Maintaining spiritual practices can rewire neurological circuits and deepen the path to nirvana. Positive psychology emphasizes virtues, gratitude, and a positive outlook, which align with spiritual ethics and mindfulness.

Finally, continuing and deepening the path to enlightenment is a complex and dynamic process that draws on ancient spiritual wisdom and modern viewpoints. Mindfulness, meditation, self-inquiry, ethical living, awareness in daily activities, surrender, community support, interconnectedness, impermanence and non-attachment, and nature attunement nourish and propel the spiritual journey.

As people move through their inner landscapes, their commitment to enlightenment becomes a sacred pilgrimage that awakens collective consciousness and evolves humanity. With each step, the trip reveals additional layers of knowledge and invites people to dance with existence's mysteries and spiritual illumination.

CONCLUSION

The writers of "Sacred Sensuality: A Guide to Sex Magic and Spiritual Awakening - Transforming Intimacy into a Path of Enlightenment," a compelling inquiry, deftly weave together the themes of sensuality, spirituality, and personal growth. This ground-breaking manual crosses traditional lines to take readers into a world where close relationships serve as a means of enlightenment and spiritual development.

The book offers profound insights into the alchemy of sexuality and spirituality as it unfolds like a mystical trip. The writers skillfully traverse the subtleties of sacred sensuality, stressing its transforming ability as a road to greater awareness through a blend of traditional wisdom and contemporary viewpoints. The main idea is summed up in the subtitle, "Transforming Intimacy into a Path of Enlightenment," which states that when intimacy is addressed with reverence and attention, it can serve as a doorway to a profound spiritual awakening.

Beyond the usual conversations about sex, the guide explores the world of sex magic and how it might accelerate spiritual development. It deftly treads the line between connection, desire, and the holy, offering readers helpful tips, customs, and meditative activities to help them incorporate sacred sensuality into their daily lives.

The book acts as a compass for readers as they set out on this trip, providing direction on negotiating the challenging terrain of close relationships. It encourages a comprehensive understanding of sensuality, highlighting its potential to go beyond the material and transform into a holy activity consistent with the larger pattern of spiritual awakening.

In summary, "Sacred Sensuality" emerges as a manifesto and a guide for elevating the commonplace to a remarkable level and uniting it with the sacred. It invites readers to follow a road where the fusion of spirituality and sensuality becomes a transformative force that leads to a higher state of enlightenment in the end. The writers invite readers to embrace the great potential in their close relationships using their perceptive prose and helpful advice, transforming the ordinary into an astonishing, spiritually enlightening trip.

Thank you for buying and reading/ listening to our book. If you found this book useful/ helpful please take a few minutes and leave a review on the platform where you purchased our book. Your feedback matters greatly to us.